Cloud Computing

Assessing the risks

Cloud Computing

Assessing the risks

JARED CARSTENSEN
BERNARD GOLDEN
JP MORGENTHAL

IT Governance Publishing

IT Governance Publishing
IT Governance Limited
Unit 3, Clive Court
Bartholomew's Walk
Cambridgeshire Business Park
Ely
Cambridgeshire
CB7 4EA
United Kingdom

www.itgovernance.co.uk

First published in the United Kingdom in 2012
by IT Governance Publishing.

ISBN: 978-1-84928-359-5

WHAT OTHERS ARE SAYING ABOUT THIS BOOK

'The single biggest barrier to the adoption of Cloud Computing is the challenge of security. Consumers have willingly traded vast troves of formerly confidential information in return for free access to social applications, but regulatory requirements imposed on enterprises, and their need to protect intellectual property and corporate data, place them at the opposite end of the spectrum. This book, written by technology and business leaders at the forefront of Cloud Computing, gets to the heart of the Cloud security debate by tackling the complex issues of Cloud security, compliance, availability and the law in a well-structured, easy-to-digest form. This book is timely and accurate, and will give anyone contemplating the adoption of Cloud-based services a new perspective on the risks and opportunities posed by this profound change in IT. I recommend this book without reservation as a powerful tool to inform decision making in any organisation contemplating the future of IT.'
Simon Crosby, CTO, Bromium (and former CTO, Citrix Cloud Computing Group)

'There can be few technologies which encapsulate the challenges facing organisations today in the use of technology better than Cloud. The competing challenges of flexibility, cost reduction, scalability and risk management all collide in this one area. This book breaks down the various components associated with Cloud in an easy-to-read business context, giving a great overview of the various topics and how those challenges collide. Most importantly, this book gives practical insight into how organisations can manage the various risks relating to a technology which will become ever more prevalent.'

Mike Maddison, Partner & Head of Enterprise Risk Services, Europe, Deloitte & Touche

'I would encourage using this book to gain a good understanding of the Cloud and the numerous variations available, following the links provided to areas of particular interest. The authors have done a sterling job of presenting the subject matter in an easy-to-follow manner, and have provided good industry examples to explain some of the key concepts.'

Raj Samani, EMEA Strategy Advisor, Cloud Security Alliance

'The term "Cloud" is synonymous with opportunity, vendor FUD and misdirection; as a result, the market for IT solutions and services involving Cloud has become almost impossible to navigate for IT departments. However, along with the opportunity and power of Cloud, comes an equal amount of risk. Without the appropriate decisions on governance, management, organisation and compliance, Cloud can quickly become an enormous risk to the business. This book provides the reader with an outstanding view of Cloud from the variety of service offerings to the unending opportunities and risks they represent. It is truly a top-down and bottom-up look at all things Cloud, and should be considered a must read for anyone getting their feet wet in the world of Cloud. Read this book, so you can enable your business, while managing the risk.'

Mark Thiele, Enterprise Vice President, Data Centre Tech, Switch

What Others Are Saying About this Book

'The book carefully analyses the current state of Cloud Computing, with a focus on the complex relationship between security, compliance and risk. It should be a most welcome read to senior stakeholders looking to embrace the new Cloud Computing wave.'

Eugene Kaspersky, Chairman and CEO,
Kaspersky Lab

'This book and its authors do a great job of clearly defining Cloud-security elements and impacts on the organisation, including executives' decision making, governance, risk and compliance angles. With examples and analogies used throughout, this book makes it both understandable and practical for all readers. The chapters focusing on Cloud forensics, impacts on the organisation, and geographical challenges make this book particularly valuable in comparison with other Cloud publications currently available. This book is a great read, and deserves a place in everyone's bookshelf who is interested in Cloud Computing!'

Christiaan Beek, Principal Consultant IR and
Forensics EMEA at Foundstone

'Remarkable work of synthesis performed by the authors. This book is a must-have for anyone willing to have both a clear and pragmatic approach, as well as a better understanding of impacts on business when dealing with Cloud Computing. "If you think education is expensive, try ignorance!" – Abraham Lincoln.'

Ludovic Petit, Chief Information Security
Officer, SFR

'This book gives a good account of defining Cloud Computing, assessing the risks and benefits in a clear, concise and impartial manner. Strong on governance and security, it is a welcome addition to both learning and customer decision making in the area. It is also of assistance in informing suppliers who are strong on technology to the range and detail of customer concerns, which are as much commercial and legal as technical. Speaking as a lawyer working in the Cloud area, I learnt a lot from reading it and will be recommending it to suppliers and customers alike. It is a most useful book.'

Pearse Ryan, Partner, Technology & Life Science Group, Arthur Cox Solicitors; Member, Cloud Industry Forum, Legal Advisory

'If you're an executive who needs to figure out how to embrace the benefits of Cloud Computing while minimising the risks, this jargon-free book is for you. Written in plain English by seasoned technology leaders, *Cloud Computing: Assessing the risks* is structured to provide both introductory and advanced concepts to the business executive. JP Morgenthal, Bernard Golden, and Jared Carstensen can take you from zero to hero in understanding the complexities of how to manage risk when working with Cloud resources. The book is comprehensive, explaining the basics like Cloud service models and implications of Cloud Computing characteristics, to more advanced topics like technical investigations in the Cloud and dealing with implications of international privacy regulations when considering a Cloud deployment. This is a useful book for managers getting up to speed on Cloud Computing, as well as a strategic overview for seasoned IT professionals who want to make sure they're considering all the implications of a transition to the Cloud.'

Gal Shpantzer, Co-founder, Security Outliers

'This publication takes the reader on a comprehensive journey through Cloud Computing security. All aspects of Cloud security are explained, from initial considerations of the impact that Cloud thinking brings to an organisation, through governance, compliance, risk awareness, security assessment, organisational liability, business continuity and compliance. Notably, the emerging topic of Cloud forensics is discussed, presenting broad and relevant coverage of the Cloud security topics that IT professionals need to know. This timely publication delivers an accessible, engaging and critical introduction to secure Cloud Computing.'

Dr Richard Hill, Head of Computing and Mathematics, University of Derby

'Cloud is the most disruptive change in computing in the past 10 years. Its emergence is fast with an all-encompassing reach that will affect all of us in some way. This book is an essential read for anyone in an IT role as an end-user, reseller or vendor. It delivers clarity of understanding, from what you need to know surrounding Cloud implementations through to great real-world explanations, including the impact on both the organisation and individuals involved. Treat reading this as a worthwhile investment in your future career.'

Ian Moyse, Board Member EuroCloud and Governance Board Member of the Cloud Industry Forum; named one of the top 200 Cloud Channel Experts in 2011 by TalkinCloud

'This book provides a good 50,000-feet view of the various elements associated with Cloud Computing, with emphasis on a security and compliance perspective. Overall, this book provides a thoughtful introduction to a complex and difficult field.'

Phil Beckett, Managing Director Forensic
Technology, Navigant Consulting

FOREWORD

'Cloud is secure!' 'Cloud is insecure!' How many times have you heard these very contrarian viewpoints argued – often by the same person – without the necessary context reinforcing these assertions or anything substantive offered beyond anecdotes and buzzwords for comparison?

It is clear that Cloud Computing has achieved escape velocity from the massive hype that initially had it tethered in low orbit to the point that it has now joined the ranks of popular culture.

Everyone, from technicians to technophobes, speak of 'The Cloud,' each with their own interpretation of why and how it matters personally. Whether you're an end-user, a small business, a large enterprise or government, Cloud Computing has something to offer everyone.

Of course, arguments still arise over the vagaries of vocabulary and the definition of 'Cloud,' and downright religious crusades have erupted with dogmatic contention offering notions of 'true' versus 'false' Cloud. Luckily, over the last few years, we have seen these discussions become more empirical and move from 'what is Cloud' to 'how can I use it?'

The business value of Cloud Computing presents tremendous potential opportunity if one is willing and able to make the technical, cultural, operational and organisational shifts necessary to get there. For some, especially this latest generation of digital natives, the Cloud (and the Internet) is the only thing they've ever known. For others, it represents an unknown and thus a potential threat to the status quo.

As Cloud Computing promises many wonderful benefits, often we witness objections and concerns raised. Many are the result of technical debt from prior paradigm shifts in computing. These 'taxes' are levied atop a vast set of consternation; security, compliance, risk and trust are always at the tip of the tongue when objections to Cloud surface.

Much of this concern stems from the dissonance between the reference models we use today and the new operational, technical and business models that Cloud brings. Divining what is the same or different can be difficult, especially when mapping a path that includes having to simultaneously support legacy approaches whilst pushing the boundaries of disruption.

The complexity, static implementations and interdependencies that exist in traditional enterprise IT and the ways in which we have approached securing and making compliant our assets are exacerbated by the agility, flexibility, dynamism, scale, self-service and mobility that Cloud Computing introduces.

In general, the community responsible for evaluating and ultimately operating the security apparatus under the unrelenting pressures of compliance and governance oversight are left wondering how to grasp the relevant differences between what they do today and what Cloud Computing brings them. In many cases, these same teams are left wondering if they have relevance at all as the so-called 'shadow IT' operates around them as their skillsets and operational models sit quietly in the corner collecting dust.

Foreword

It is true, however, that static, faith-based security, compliance and risk management solutions will not cut it in the dynamic and high-velocity world of Cloud Computing. We must adapt operationally to ensure that the way in which we measure, assess and attest the security, compliance and governance of our businesses stand as equals in the dynamic and agile world of Cloud.

Leveraging a common sense approach that clearly highlights the pros and cons of Cloud Computing with respect to offering rational guidance across a vast landscape of security, compliance, governance and risk concerns is sorely needed.

What great luck it is then, that you have such a guide at your fingertips in this book!

I have had the great pleasure of personally interacting with the authors and reading many of their musings over the last few years relating to Cloud Computing. When I was asked to write the foreword to this book, I leapt at the opportunity. This book represents not just Bernard's, JP's and Jared's own opinions but the valuable insight, observation, experiences and lessons learned from consultative engagements in which they have helped guide many to success in their initial journey to embrace Cloud Computing.

I am convinced that you will find equal delight in absorbing the sage advice and pragmatic guidance that the team offers in this book and look forward to seeing it perched on the shelves amongst my other go-to guides for Cloud Computing.

To the Cloud!

Christofer Hoff

ABOUT THE AUTHORS

Jared Carstensen is an internationally recognised and renowned information security specialist working for Deloitte & Touche. He is a certified industry professional by the International Information Systems Security Consortium (ISC)^2, Information Systems Audit and Control Association (ISACA), British Standards Institute (BSI), Cloud Security Alliance (CSA), City & Guilds, and the NCC (UK).

Jared has contributed and led projects for numerous Fortune 500 companies, government and state bodies, financial institutions, large multinationals, intelligence and law enforcements bodies, and blue-chip firms around the world. These include projects in Ireland, the United Kingdom, the United Arab Emirates, Nigeria, South Africa and the United States. Jared has also led a number of highly complex flagship projects in West Africa, South Africa and the United States.

He regularly contributes as a member of the following organisations – International Information Systems Security Consortium (ISC)^2, Information Systems Audit and Control Association (ISACA), the British Standards Institute (BSI), and Standards.org.

Jared has been a featured speaker at numerous international events on security and best-practice related topics, and was selected as a member of the IT Governance Expert Panel (10+ Domains) and an advisory panel member for Standards.org.

Bernard Golden has been called a 'Cloud guru'. He is the CEO of HyperStratus, a Silicon Valley Cloud Computing consultancy which works with clients in the US and throughout the world. The firm's clients include Korea Telecom, Chunghwa Telecom, Pepsi and BMC Software. HyperStratus provides Cloud Computing services in the areas of application security, system architecture and design, TCO analysis and project implementation.

Bernard is the Cloud Computing Advisor for *CIO Magazine*. His blog has been called 'brilliant and incisive' and is read by tens of thousands of people each month. It was named 'Top 50 Cloud Computing Blog' by Sys-Con Media, a '20 Most Important Cloud Blog' by AlwaysOn Media, and in a recent poll by AppDynamics his was cited as the third most influential Cloud Computing blog. In a recent study, he was described as a Top 100 'Most Powerful Voice' in security. Bernard's writings on Cloud Computing have also been published by *The New York Times* and the *Harvard Business Review*.

Bernard is the author of *Virtualisation for Dummies* (Wiley, 2007), the most popular book on the subject ever published. He is also the co-author of *Creating the Infrastructure for Cloud Computing* (Intel Press, 2011). Bernard is a popular and engaging presenter, and has keynoted conferences from Moscow to Peru.

JP Morgenthal is one of the world's foremost experts in IT strategy and Cloud Computing. He has over 25 years of expertise applying emerging technology to complex business problems. JP has strong business acumen complemented by technical depth and breadth. He is a respected author on topics of integration, software development and Cloud Computing and is the lead Cloud

Computing Editor for InfoQ. In 2002, JP was named one of the leading CTOs on B2B and continues to demonstrate how technology can drive business value. He has been in corporate IT, worked as an industry analyst on middleware, and as a software executive. His book *Enterprise Information Integration: A Pragmatic Approach* (Lulu.com, 2005) foresaw the coming of the API industry for data integration.

ACKNOWLEDGEMENTS

From the authors we would like to thank the fantastic team at IT Governance Publishing (Vicki, Sophie, Angela), the editors, all of the reviewers and industry experts who have been kind enough to provide endorsements for this book – thank you so much! Your time and efforts on this are really appreciated.

Thanks to Chris Evans DPSM MBCS and ir H.L. (Maarten Souw) RE, IT-Auditor, UWV for reviewing the manuscript.

We would also like to thank you the reader for choosing this book! We hope you find this book useful, educational and insightful – whatever your reasons for choosing it. If you find this book of benefit, please pay us the ultimate compliment and recommend it to someone who may find it useful. Our goal from the start was to share insights, experiences, knowledge and information with the view to assisting anyone in the Cloud space.

Again – thank you!

The authors

Acknowledgements

I would like to thank all the team at ITGP who came to us with the idea, and for their fantastic work throughout.

Also I would like to thank the fantastic Bernard Golden and JP Morgenthal for their amazing work and contributions! This book would not be the same without you guys!

Finally, I would like to thank the love of my life, Tonya, and my fantastic family Sonja, Clive and Brent for always supporting, inspiring and encouraging me in everything I do. Thank you all so much!

Jared Carstensen

To Alison, Sebastian and Oliver: three glorious stars in the Golden sky.

Bernard Golden

I would like to thank my co-authors, Jared Carstensen and Bernard Golden, for launching this project and so graciously inviting my participation.

Also, I would like to thank the people at IT Governance, Angela Wilde and Vicki Utting, for their assistance in bringing this publication to market.

Finally, I would like to thank my wife, Amy, and my children, Amanda and Daniel, for continuing to inspire me to be the best I can be.

JP Morgenthal

CONTENTS

Contents

Contents

CHAPTER 1: CLOUD COMPUTING EXPLAINED

The potential of Cloud Computing

In late 2007, executives at *The New York Times* faced a common commercial dilemma: they identified an attractive business opportunity, but couldn't pursue it because of the high cost and long lead time for necessary IT resources. Initial estimates for the project were that it would require over $100,000 investment and couldn't start for several months' time due to the lengthy timeframe for budget request, hardware ordering and installation/configuration.

It's no secret that the newspaper business is severely challenged by the growth of the Internet. Any new profitable business offerings capable of increasing subscriber loyalty are eagerly seized by an industry worried about falling revenues and fickle readers.

The project at hand was designed to take advantage of *The Times*' historic position as the 'newspaper of record' for the United States. Archives of the paper from 1851 to 1922 had been digitised, and *The Times* wished to make images of the pages available over the Web.

Unfortunately, the existing digital scans were in the TIFF format, which were too large to serve over the Web. The original scans needed to be converted – but large amounts of computing power would be needed, requiring significant capital investment (over $100,000) and time to fund, procure, install and configure (six months or more).

While the organisation chewed over how to proceed, Derek Gottfrid, a *Times* software engineer, pursued a different course of action. Having heard about Amazon Web

Services (AWS) and its Infrastructure-as-a-Service offering, Derek uploaded all four terabytes of the TIFF images to the Amazon Simple Storage Service (S3). He then started 100 virtual machines in the Amazon Elastic Compute Cloud (EC2), on which he installed the popular Hadoop parallel processing software. Over the course of a single weekend, Derek's program read files from S3, converted the images in one of the 100 EC2 instances, and then wrote the converted images back to S3. When the job was complete, he shut down the virtual machines and released the compute capacity back to AWS. Total cost? $240. And, by the way, *The Times* continues to use S3 as the storage for the files and serves user requests for the images directly from AWS.

Even the briefest look at this example indicates the tremendous potential for Cloud Computing. Who wouldn't choose right now over 'months from now'? Who wouldn't select $240 rather than $100,000 plus?

But a single swallow does not a summer make, nor does a single example describe the totality of Cloud Computing. In order to understand the promise and peril of Cloud Computing, it's important to get a full picture of Cloud Computing: in other words, what is Cloud Computing – or, put another way, how may Cloud Computing be defined?

Cloud Computing defined

Sometimes it seems that there are more definitions of Cloud Computing than there are stars in the sky. Certainly there are hundreds of definitions bandied about by vendors, journalists, IT personnel, pundits and public relations representatives. However, one definition stands out as authoritative: that of the National Institute of Standards and Testing (NIST), an agency within the United States Department of Commerce that is charged with developing standards and measures on behalf of the United States Federal Government.

The NIST Cloud Computing definition (available at *http://csrc.nist.gov/publications/nistpubs/800-145/SP800-145.pdf*) has three sections:

1 Essential characteristics. NIST identifies five characteristics that a Cloud Computing environment must embody to implement 'true' Cloud Computing. The five characteristics are:
   - On-demand self-service
   - Broad network access
   - Resource pooling
   - Rapid elasticity
   - Measured service.

2 Service models. NIST defines three ways that Cloud Computing may be delivered:
   - Cloud Software-as-a-Service
   - Cloud Platform-as-a-Service
   - Cloud Infrastructure-as-a-Service.

3 Deployment models. NIST describes four different ways that Cloud Computing environments can be deployed:
   - Private Cloud
   - Community Cloud
   - Public Cloud
   - Hybrid Cloud.

Much of the discussion about Cloud Computing centres around the deployment models, so it is worthwhile examining how Cloud Computing can be deployed before moving on to the characteristics and delivery models.

Cloud Computing deployment models

Private Cloud is one in which the Cloud infrastructure is operated solely for an organisation. It may be managed by the organisation or a third party and may exist on or off premises.

Essentially, a private Cloud is one dedicated to the use of one organisation; it has full use of all of the Cloud environment's resources and also bears full responsibility for its costs.

Community Cloud is one in which the Cloud infrastructure is shared by several organisations and supports a specific community that has shared concerns (e.g. mission, security requirements, policy, and compliance considerations). It may be managed by the organisations or a third party and may exist on or off premises.

A community Cloud would commonly be domain-specific (e.g. a Cloud dedicated to use by government health organisations) and operated on behalf of organisations with common objectives and operations.

Public Cloud is a form of Cloud in which the Cloud infrastructure is made available to the general public or a large industry group and is owned by an organisation selling Cloud services.

A public Cloud is available for use by anyone who cares to use it and no commonality of use patterns, application type or user profile is assumed.

Hybrid Cloud describes a deployment situation where the Cloud infrastructure is a composition of two or more Clouds (private, community or public) that remain unique entities but are bound together by standardised or proprietary technology that enables data and application portability (e.g. Cloud bursting for load balancing between Clouds).

It is important to note that hybrid Cloud is the deployment model that is most ambiguous in common use, with the term used to describe very different Cloud topologies and use patterns. For example, the NIST definition implies that a hybrid Cloud is made up of two or more deployment environments, both of which must be Cloud environments.

By contrast, many people use the term 'hybrid Cloud' to describe an environment in which applications may be deployed internally in a traditional corporate data centre or to an external private or public Cloud environment – in other words, to these people a hybrid Cloud deployment model does not require multiple Cloud environments.

When discussing or reading about hybrid Cloud, one must be extremely careful to understand the assumptions another party has about what qualifies as a hybrid Cloud, as the implications of the different versions of hybrid are quite different.

Another important aspect of deployment model to keep in mind is the difference between private and public Cloud Computing environments. Specifically, with regard to security and compliance, many people assume that public Cloud environments present significant risk, while private Cloud environments are immune to risk from these factors.

While it is true that private and public Cloud environments differ and present different risk profiles, it is not the case that risk is entirely associated with public Cloud deployment environments, while private Cloud environments are immune to risk.

This book will discuss the risks associated with Cloud Computing in general, and the specific risks associated with the public and private deployment models; but make no mistake, risk is present in any form of computing and Cloud Computing is no exception, no matter which deployment model is implemented.

Cloud Computing service models

The NIST definition identifies three Cloud Computing service models: Infrastructure-as-a-Service, Platform-as-a-Service and Software-as-a-Service. The so-called 'IPS' taxonomy to define Cloud Computing service models is typical throughout the IT industry, and definitely provides a convenient method to understand how a given Cloud offering fits into the larger Cloud Computing picture.

It's worthwhile to review the NIST definition of each service model before delving into what each service model implies.

Cloud Software-as-a-Service (SaaS) The capability provided to the consumer is to use the provider's applications running on a Cloud infrastructure. The applications are accessible from various client devices through a thin client interface such as a web browser (e.g. web-based e-mail). The consumer does not manage or control the underlying Cloud infrastructure including network, servers, operating systems, storage or even individual application capabilities, with the possible exception of limited user-specific application configuration settings.

Cloud Platform-as-a-Service (PaaS) The capability provided to the consumer is to deploy onto the Cloud infrastructure consumer-created or acquired applications created using programming languages and tools supported by the provider. The consumer does not manage or control the underlying Cloud infrastructure including network, servers, operating systems or storage, but has control over the deployed applications and possibly application hosting environment configurations.

Cloud Infrastructure-as-a-Service (IaaS) The capability provided to the consumer is to provision processing, storage, networks and other fundamental computing resources where the consumer is able to deploy and run arbitrary software, which can include operating systems and applications. The consumer does not manage or control the underlying Cloud infrastructure but has control over operating systems, storage, deployed applications and possibly limited control of selected networking components (e.g. host firewalls).

Discussion of each service model

While the NIST definition goes through a progression of SaaS, PaaS and IaaS, we will describe the service models in a different order: IaaS, SaaS and PaaS. We do this for clarity, as the description of each of the models can best be understood when addressed in this order.

Infrastructure-as-a-Service The best way to think about IaaS is that it offers the ability to use fundamental computing resources like virtual machines or network capacity on an as-needed basis. The using organisation does not own the capital assets (i.e. the physical servers or network switches, which are owned by the service provider), but merely uses the computing capacity offered by those assets.

The most common way of paying for these resources is on a 'pay-as-you-go' model; that is, a rental model in which payment is made for a granular use of the service. For example, IaaS virtual machines are commonly offered for a per-hour fee, with the fee tied to the capacity of the virtual machine. A small machine might be, say, $0.10 per hour, while one with four times the capacity might be $0.40 per hour.

The benefit of IaaS is that it breaks the previous necessity of owning computing assets in order to perform computing processes. While ownership of an asset is often the best way to get the greatest possible benefit from it, in other use cases, ownership is uneconomic. That is why we rent cars at vacation destinations rather than purchasing a new car every time we visit a new holiday spot.

The problem with many computing tasks in organisations is that they are poorly suited for the asset ownership model. Owning a large amount of computing infrastructure to manage the once-a-month accounting reconciliation is an example where owning computing assets is poorly matched to the use profile; the remainder of the month, where no reconciliation is going on, represents a waste of capital as those assets sit idle. Likewise, occasional analytic processing represents another poor computer utilisation situation. IaaS offers the opportunity to rent computing resources for short periods of time to manage occasional or peak workloads.

In addition to the obvious use cases associated with temporary computing resource use, some organisations have moved to use IaaS for use cases associated with ongoing computing. For example, Netflix uses Amazon Web Services to host its main website and much of its order processing and digital media management. Even though Netflix is certainly capable of managing its own technology infrastructure, it prefers to rely on Amazon to build and operate data centres and computing infrastructure, since Amazon specialises in this. Offloading this aspect of its online service allows Netflix to concentrate in areas it sees as its core differentiator: media delivery, recommendation engine and supply chain management.

There is also some evidence that IaaS providers can deliver their compute services less expensively than IT organisations can with their own assets. For those IT organisations, it's less expensive to use an external provider than attempt to own and operate their own computing infrastructure. Significant controversy about whether internal assets or external Clouds are less expensive exists, and no universally accepted answer is available. However, there is a trend by many companies to move a sizable portion of their computing to external Cloud service providers. Naturally, one of the concerns raised about putting important compute workloads in an external provider is security, which will be addressed at length in the remainder of this book.

Software-as-a-Service   The best way to think of the SaaS service model is as an application delivered over the Internet, with the using organisation taking on no responsibility for application deployment or operation. The SaaS provider retains control and, ultimately, obligation for all aspects of application delivery – availability, performance and, of course, security.

By contrast, the using organisation bears no responsibility for the application's service characteristics – users merely interact with the application.

One other aspect of SaaS is quite critical, though not overtly described in the service model definition. SaaS applications are typically not dedicated to a single user organisation, the way an on-premises application usually is. The sharing of a single application by many different user organisations is commonly referred to as multi-tenancy. The fact that many different organisations – indeed, even competitors – share a single application, raises the importance of application security and partitioning the application design, so that one user cannot see the data of a second user from a different organisation.

SaaS applications are quite different from the traditional on-premises variety, and offer many benefits.

First and foremost, the using organisation does not need to pay a large software licence fee upfront and has no need to invest in software or hardware. Moreover, the organisation does not need to devote any personnel (or hire external system integrators) to implement and configure the application.

As a second benefit, avoiding this investment and need to assemble internal or external personnel can, in many cases, speed application deployment, as the SaaS application is available for use immediately.

A third benefit is related to the licence fee avoidance already mentioned. Most SaaS applications are paid for on a subscription basis; the most common form is a monthly fee per user. Subscription payments more closely ties actual use (and, one hopes, benefit) to the financial investment associated with application use, thereby getting more value from the application.

Platform-as-a-Service PaaS occupies a middle ground between IaaS and SaaS. In a PaaS environment, the Cloud provider offers a framework for users to create and operate applications. PaaS frameworks provide libraries that application programmers can use to install and run code, store data, manage user identity and a whole host of useful application services.

Why PaaS is important can be understood by looking at the fourth Cloud Computing characteristic: 'Capabilities can be rapidly and elastically provisioned, in some cases automatically, to scale rapidly outward and inward commensurate with demand.' This so-called autoscaling does not occur 'automagically'; in IaaS environments the application and the application management framework must be configured to implement it. Moreover, it is typically necessary to design and program the application itself to ensure that it adds and subtracts computing resources as needed. This means that the application developer must devote time to implement this functionality, diverting effort away from the businesss logic of the application. A final problem in this scenario is that implementing this autoscaling functionality in an application is not simple, and many software engineers do not have the required ability.

The PaaS environment addresses these issues by making the Cloud provider responsible for the infrastructure portions of the capability, freeing the application developer to focus on business logic – which is presumably the point of the application. In a PaaS environment, the Cloud provider takes responsibility for ensuring infrastructure services (e.g. data storage) are abstracted from specific hardware and are capable of operating at scale. Unlike IaaS environments, where the application creator is responsible for adding additional resources like virtual machines if the application load grows, in a PaaS environment, the application creator can rely on the PaaS provider to take care of those details – which allows the creator to focus on the functionality of the application.

One might say that PaaS enables application developers to avoid dealing with the 'plumbing' of applications – virtual machine connectivity and security, infrastructure logic to allow additional resources to be added or removed from the application topology, and so on.

To this point in the evolution of Cloud Computing, PaaS has been underused, in part because the other delivery models have proved to be immediately adopted, but also because the early PaaS offerings were relatively immature.

Since the beginning of 2011, however, a number of PaaS offerings have come to market and hold great promise to increase PaaS adoption. The functionality of these PaaS offerings is broader than earlier offerings, with additional services targeted at complete business application functionality as part of the interface.

For example, several of the newer PaaS offerings come with interfaces for billing, making it simpler for application developers to implement pay-as-you-go or chargeback pricing models.

It may be expected that PaaS Cloud Computing will become much more popular and widely adopted. The productivity benefits of leveraging services rather than having to implement service functionality for every new application are attractive. Furthermore, enabling application developers to focus on business functionality rather than plumbing makes PaaS more attractive to those drawn to Cloud Computing for business agility reasons.

Key characteristics of Cloud Computing

By far the most revolutionary part of NIST's Cloud Computing definition lies in the five characteristics it identifies as core to Cloud Computing.

It is absolutely critical that any person interested in Cloud Computing and how it may be applied, understands these five characteristics – and, more importantly, understands the implication of these five characteristics.

The following discussion will take each characteristic in turn and discuss its meaning and implications.

Characteristic One: On-demand self-service

The first Cloud Computing characteristic is defined by NIST as:

A consumer can unilaterally provision computing capabilities, such as server time and network storage, as needed automatically without requiring human interaction with each service's provider.

What this means is that a consumer controls the provisioning process and does not need to interact with anyone or submit a request for approval in order to obtain computing resources. More directly, this means developers (consumers does not refer to the ultimate end-users of an application, but rather to someone associated with creating or operating the application that runs on the Cloud infrastructure) can obtain resources without going to the IT operations and infrastructure group. The developer 'self-serves' and directly chooses resources, which are automatically delivered to him or her.

The vision embodied in this characteristic is something like what one experiences in Amazon.com's purchase process: a resource (product) one desires is identified, a web-based form is filled out, necessary checks are performed (e.g. is a valid credit card on file for the user), and the transaction is automatically completed.

Implications of Characteristic One

The immediate and obvious implication of this characteristic is that it transfers control and power from IT operations to application developers.

Operations no longer acts as a gatekeeper to computing resources, doling them out upon request. A less pleasant description of this process is that developers no longer have to suffer having to justify a request for resources to a member of an organisation that feels its charter is to ration access to precious resources. In an influential report on Cloud Computing, the UC Berkeley RAD Lab (Reliable Adaptive Distributed Systems Laboratory) describes Cloud Computing as providing 'the illusion of infinite resources', indicating how far this world is from the traditional perception of IT resources as expensive and limited.

Even without the aspersion regarding the self-appointed resource rationing role of IT operations, the self-service nature of Cloud Computing obviously reduces the friction that accompanies the traditional mode of resource acquisition. This is a complementary implication to the self-service characteristic: when the friction associated with obtaining resources drops, people will request more resources. In fact, one may expect the demand for computing resources to skyrocket as a result of the self-service nature of Cloud Computing. This is not the only implication of on-demand self-service for Cloud Computing, however.

A second implication of the on-demand self-service characteristic is that automated policy and governance regarding resource requests must be in place. Traditionally, the resource request was forwarded to an operations system administrator, who knew the organisation's rules for who was approved to request resources and who did not have the requisite permission to obtain resources. In other words, a great deal of organisation policy was held by system administrators as tacit knowledge, applied to specific requests.

In the on-demand self-service world, though, there is no point at which a human system administrator intervenes in the process. Something must be in place to implement the tacit knowledge formerly applied by a system administrator – and that something is automated policy rules applied to resource request submissions. So an automated policy engine capable of capturing the rules of the organisation regarding resource requests is necessary to support the characteristic of on-demand self-service.

A third implication of on-demand self-service is the dramatic foreshortening of the insight infrastructure and operations (I&O) groups have into resource demand. The job of capacity planning becomes much, much more difficult in the world of Cloud Computing.

In the past, I&O groups would learn of upcoming server provisioning requests well ahead of time. When an application required hardware to host software, a budget request for the capital expense would be submitted, alerting every group involved in the provisioning process that additional server demand was on the horizon.

Today, by contrast, a developer can submit a resource request via a self-service portal and receive that resource within just a few minutes – and the I&O groups are expected to deliver. The obvious implication is that little future visibility about resource demand is available; a less obvious, but still critical, implication is that I&O is expected to have sufficient capacity available at all times to meet resource requests, and that application groups will operate as though sufficient resources will be available.

This characteristic means the traditional relationship between application and I&O groups is upended – instead of application groups asking well ahead of time and I&O groups doling out precious resources if the request meets the approved criteria, in a Cloud world application, groups will submit requests according to their own judgement about request validity and I&O groups will be expected to deliver immediately. Certainly the traditional power relationship between the two groups shifts dramatically as a result of the self-service characteristic of Cloud Computing.

Characteristic Two: Broad network access

The second Cloud Computing characteristic is defined by NIST as:

Capabilities are available over the network and accessed through standard mechanisms that promote use by heterogeneous thin or thick client platforms (e.g. mobile phones, tablets, laptops and workstations).

This characteristic speaks directly to the methods by which Cloud Computing applications interact with Cloud Computing infrastructures and applications, and indirectly to what we may expect as to likely demand profiles.

In terms of the methods by which interactions in Cloud environments take place, this characteristic means that users may expect widely used standard mechanisms to be in place to support communication. Proprietary protocols designed to limit device type or impose need for licensing fees or royalty payments are not acceptable in the Cloud Computing world.

Instead, common protocols like HTTP are expected to be used as the basis for communication and connectivity. This enables any device that supports those protocols to be integrated into the application environment. Furthermore, it eases the effort required to add a new device into an application environment – as long as the device supports the appropriate protocols, it easily integrates.

The NIST definition of this characteristic mentions mobile phones and tablets, but omits an extremely important source of Cloud interaction – communication from other computer programs. Instead of humans using a device to interact with a Cloud environment, the standard protocols may be used by other computer programs to interact with the environment. Common types of external programs interacting with Cloud environments include: (1) other tools that co-ordinate the Cloud application, causing it to perform some action; (2) applications that call a Cloud-based service and integrate its output into the application; and (3) applications residing in specialised hardware devices (e.g. a smart electric meter) that connect to a Cloud-based application and submit or retrieve data.

It's easy to underestimate the role these sources of traffic play in the Cloud world. One example should indicate how large this type of traffic is in Cloud Computing: at a recent conference, a representative of Salesforce stated that of the 500 million daily page views its application serves up, fully 50% of them are served up in response to calls made to the Salesforce API, rather than to the Salesforce client interface.

Implications of Characteristic Two

The Salesforce example serves to illustrate the indirect effect that use of standard interface protocols will have. Simply put, demand loads on Cloud applications will be significantly higher than most people expect. Extrapolating from load profiles of traditional applications primarily oriented toward human interaction is inappropriate, given how standard protocols and API interfaces encourage innovation in interaction methods.

One sees that just as the reduced friction of resource acquisition via self-service will increase overall demand enormously, so too will interfaces and protocols that support additional traffic from untraditional sources like other applications and specialised devices.

The vastly increased load that will occur as a result of this characteristic will, of course, increase demand for computing resources. This increase in demand will exacerbate the challenge of capacity planning described in the previously discussed Characteristic One, above.

Characteristic Three: Resource pooling

The third Cloud Computing characteristic identified is defined by NIST as:

The provider's computing resources are pooled to serve multiple consumers using a multi-tenant model, with different physical and virtual resources dynamically assigned and reassigned according to consumer demand. There is a sense of location independence in that the customer generally has no control or knowledge over the exact location of the provided resources but may be able to specify location at a higher level of abstraction (e.g. country, state or data centre). Examples of resources include storage, processing, memory and network bandwidth.

A common pattern regarding resources in IT organisations today is that different departments pay for and control their own compute resources. In other words, the HR department pays for its servers, the finance group for its servers, and so on. This mode can lead to poor resource utilisation: one group's resources can be overwhelmed with load, affecting application SLA, while on the next rack over, another group's resources may be standing by idle, with no load to speak of.

An example of this situation is at the end of each month, when the finance department's servers are pegged at capacity, trying to update the company's income statement, while nearby the HR department's servers run at less than five per cent load.

Cloud Computing does away with the world of dedicated resources and substitutes an environment where the resources are shared among all groups, dynamically assigned according to the needs of the moment – and then reassigned later to yet another user, all based on how much resource is required for the applications to operate efficiently.

Obviously, this has the potential for making IT resource utilisation significantly more efficient. Moreover, it allows a more comprehensive approach to total resource provisioning, allowing total capacity demand to be managed at the IT organisation level, rather than demand being addressed at the individual application level.

Certainly, the ability to address one group's occasional need for additional resources (e.g. the finance department's month-end closing) through shifting other, unused resources instead of purchasing additional equipment to meet that occasional demand is attractive. It also holds the potential for reducing overall spend, as shifting demand can be met by multiplexing resource assignment across the total pool instead of buying sufficient equipment to meet each group's peak demand, thereby assuring huge waste as each group owns equipment that sits unused most of the time.

Implications of Characteristic Three

One implication of this characteristic has just been addressed – the move of budgeting from individual projects to the centralised group providing the resource pool. The benefit of sharing resources among many users can be seen across all domains of life: municipal pools, telephone switching central offices, rental cars in common travel destinations and so on.

However, other implications of resource pooling may not be so obvious.

For a start, even though sharing common resources can be more efficient, not every group using the resources may be satisfied by the arrangement.

If a group is concerned that its requirements will not be met by a shared environment, it may resist moving to it, notwithstanding the theoretical (or even practical) benefits of doing so.

There may be ego or prestige associated with 'owning' a set of resources instead of using a shared pool. Consequently, IT customers may resist having 'their' resources in a common pool.

And, even though the benefit of using a common budget to purchase resources may be undeniable, some organisations may avoid devoting their budget to a common shared resources because of concern that other organisations may 'free ride' on their budget contribution.

These are all reasons why organisations that use or contribute budget to a central pool of resources might resist doing so. However, the challenge of resource pooling must also be looked at from the perspective of the provider of the pool. For the Cloud service provider, building and offering a resource pool imposes utilisation risk.

Simply stated, utilisation risk represents the risk an organisation that provides a resource faces when trying to match supply to demand. Any Cloud provider makes a significant investment, with the expectation that use will reach the necessary levels to justify the investment. Should total demand (utilisation) of the pooled resource fall short, the Cloud provider will suffer financially.

For an internal IT group, utilisation risk is something new; in the past, individual user groups funded the equipment necessary to run their applications, making those groups responsible for appropriate capacity planning. If they miscalculated and over-purchased, the problem was theirs.

On the other hand, seen from the perspective of the overall company, this underutilisation was financially problematic – it represented a waste of corporate capital. Therefore, a shift to a shared resource pool addresses this issue, but making one pool available that is sized to meet the sum total of resource demand, thereby avoiding the wasted capacity associated with individual application resource purchase.

However, as noted, centralising the pool of resources makes the provider responsible for making use efficient – after all, if the utilisation is no higher than with the old system, why shift to a Cloud environment? This means that one key responsibility for any Cloud provider is to manage demand very carefully to ensure appropriate resource load levels.

It can seen, then, that resource pooling offers the opportunity to better balance supply with demand, multiplex demand across larger pools of users and achieve higher efficiency in terms of load. It also poses the challenge of utilisation risk, imposing responsibilities upon the Cloud provider – responsibilities that, in many cases, represent a new challenge that IT groups may never have confronted before.

Characteristic Four: Rapid elasticity

The fourth Cloud Computing characteristic is defined by NIST as:

Capabilities can be elastically provisioned and released, in some cases automatically, to scale rapidly outward and inward commensurate with demand. To the consumer, the capabilities available for provisioning often appear to be unlimited and can be appropriated in any quantity at any time.

People often underestimate how critical this characteristic is to the way Cloud Computing operates in real-world environments. Moreover, they often fail to understand the implications of this characteristic – but fully comprehending this characteristic is fundamental to grasping the opportunity afforded by Cloud Computing – as well as recognising the immense challenge Cloud Computing represents to the traditional IT world.

Rapid and elastic provisioning refers to nothing more than the ability of a user (remember, the very first characteristic of Cloud Computing is user self-service) to obtain computing resources quickly – in the order of minutes, rather than the traditional six weeks or more of provisioning time typical of most IT organisations.

Obviously, this characteristic is welcome to resource users. Being able to commence work within minutes can raise efficiency and enable application groups to respond to business conditions extremely rapidly.

Application developers are especially appreciative of this Cloud Computing characteristic. Because development commonly requires putting up compute resources and then taking them back down, a quick way to obtain resources makes a developer's job much easier. This is especially the case with complex application topologies, in which an application may be comprised of multiple tiers and multiple servers in each tier. Rapid access to the resources needed to instantiate such a topology is very useful.

In a production environment, rapid access to computing resources is also very useful. If an application experiences high load levels, being able add resources quickly makes it possible to ensure applications run at appropriate service levels and avoid unhappy users.

Implications of Characteristic Four

While the benefits of rapid elasticity are intuitively attractive, the challenges the characteristic represents are not so clear – but there are significant challenges associated with this characteristic, make no mistake.

For one thing, note the phrase 'in some cases automatically' in the first sentence of the characteristic. This is commonly understood to refer to the possibility that applications may monitor their own performance or resource demands and, on their own, with no human intervention of any sort, request additional resources necessary to operate properly. If one thought capacity planning would be more difficult in an environment in which users could request resources with no interaction with the resource provider, imagine how difficult it is in an environment in which no human has any awareness at all about resource demand!

A second implication of rapid elasticity may be seen in the 'scale rapidly outward and inward' part of this characteristic. This phrase reinforces the fact that resource users carry no commitment to specific resources beyond the point they are needed and can return the resources back to the provider with no further commitment or responsibility. This phrase further indicates the extent to which the provider carries utilisation risk in a Cloud Computing environment.

A final implication of this characteristic is carried by the portion of the definition that states 'the capabilities available for provisioning often appear to be unlimited and can be appropriated in any quantity at any time'. Put another way, this part of the characteristic definition indicates the responsibility the provider carries to make as much computing capacity that any user may desire available at all times, notwithstanding the level of resource demand currently being represented by all other users of the resource pool.

The UC Berkeley RAD Lab described this aspect of elasticity as 'the illusion of infinite capacity', meaning that every user of a Cloud environment should believe that, no matter how much computing capacity that user should need, it will always be available.

A moment's reflection should reveal how challenging this aspect of Cloud Computing is – it commits the Cloud provider to always being open for business, so to speak, and never turning anyone away. In practice, demand limitation is common; for example, even the largest Cloud provider, Amazon Web Services, imposes a limit of 20 virtual machines, but it also makes it possible to obtain more resources for any user who may need them. In one celebrated situation, Amazon provided over 5,000 virtual machine instances to a company whose online service had been featured on the front page of Facebook.

Between the two challenges of utilisation risk and 'infinite capacity', it should be clear that successfully operating a Cloud Computing environment is not for the faint-hearted.

Characteristic Five: Measured service

The fifth Cloud Computing characteristic is defined by NIST as:

Cloud systems automatically control and optimise resource use by leveraging a metering capability at some level of abstraction appropriate to the type of service (e.g. storage, processing, bandwidth and active user accounts). Resource usage can be monitored, controlled and reported, providing transparency for both the provider and consumer of the utilised service.

This NIST Cloud Computing characteristics is by far the most controversial, as it represents a huge change to how most IT organisations charge for their services, as well as an enormous challenge to implement, should the IT organisation attempt to fully comply with the characteristic. Moreover, as this characteristic focuses on money and finance, traditionally the most compelling of topics to humans, it garners immediate attention from everyone.

Having outlined a world of user self-service, transient commitment, lack of direct responsibility (i.e. the resources are held in a pool rather than being associated with a particular user), and easy and infinite availability, the question becomes, how is this paid for?

For NIST, the answer is that resource use is monitored and reported, thereby making it easy for resource users to evaluate their use patterns and respond appropriately. If use reporting indicates use that is too heavy, the resource user can decide to dial back the amount of resource being applied to its applications. Likewise, should additional resources be required to respond to changing application load, it is easy for a user to understand the amount of resource required to maintain application response times.

One obvious question is what use is made of this information obtained by metering? NIST is somewhat opaque on this topic, but there are two possibilities: (1) the metered use information is passed back to the using organisation, so that they may evaluate its meaning; or (2) the metering information may be associated with the cost required to deliver the resources and the cost may be levied upon the using organisation.

The common phrase for this second option is chargeback, meaning that the costs associated with providing a service are imposed, or charged back to the organisation using the resources. The phrase often used for the first is 'showback', meaning that resource users are shown what the level of resource use is.

Many IT organisations indicate they plan to implement showback as part of their internal Cloud efforts. In part, this may be because most IT organisations do not have sufficient information – and at the required level of granularity – to provide fine-grained billing on all elements of IT infrastructure. In many companies, information about IT resources is tracked in different budgets and even associated with different organisations. For example, servers may be operated by personnel reporting up to the CIO and, therefore, on their budget, while the power to run the servers is paid for by facilities, which reports to the CFO. Attempting to merge all of these different budget items is problematic, to say the least.

Implications of Characteristic Five

It is difficult to overestimate the implications of characteristic five – the move to measured service. Simply put, money is one of the most effective means to guide human behaviour – and changing the way money changes hands is extremely unsettling and disruptive.

Because Cloud Computing offers the opportunity to change application computing use from an 'always on' environment to an 'on when you need it, off when you don't' environment', the traditional methods of pricing use – full asset allocation, depreciated over time – are inadequate. It's vital to devise a financial accounting method that aligns with the usage model that Cloud Computing enables.

Our belief is that the showback as a mode of measuring service will have a short lifespan and be rapidly discarded in favour of direct billing for use of resources.

The transition from asset billing to measured use pricing is unlikely to be seamless. The move to measured pricing will require these actions to take place:

- All IT costs captured into a single financial structure, so that the true overall cost of IT can be applied across the resource users. Since it's common that multiple organisations have responsibility for different elements of 'IT', integrating the different budget items will require an integration effort among the different organisations. Anyone who has ever drawn up budgets understands how challenging this can be.
- Developing standardised technology offerings associated with the move to measured pricing. Many IT organisations today treat every request for resources as a 'one-off', custom designed and manually implemented. Measured services demand standardised offerings, so that pricing may be automatically applied, and standardised offerings require a move away from customised service. While a menu-based set of offerings is intuitively attractive, and certainly can reduce provisioning time, it also reduces choice. Developing standardised offerings will present a challenge to both IT and application groups.
- Moving resource consumers to measured service and direct chargeback. While measured service is intuitively attractive, asset cost assignment has the undeniable advantage of simplicity. Migrating application groups

who have traditionally made a budget transfer once or perhaps annually to a form of payment that occurs more frequently and also varies will undoubtedly be disruptive. Especially troubling to application groups will be the fact that the costs will vary according to factors that may not be explicitly chosen by the group – in other words, the cost may change according to how heavily used the system is, and that may reflect decisions by end-users. Receiving a bill predicated on decisions made by others – who may not even work for the same company – will be enormously disruptive to those paying for the service. IT groups can expect to devote significant resources to explaining the basis for chargeback costs, and those discussions may be quite heated as chargeback begins its implementation life cycle.

Long term, the move to measured service – and the inevitable complementary move to direct chargeback for resource consumption – will profoundly affect the way applications are architected and operated. Just as the increased cost of gasoline and concern about global warming have resulted in vehicles with engines that shut down when in idling situations, so too will applications begin to reduce resource consumption when dictated by low load levels.

This may prove to be the most profound effect of the move to measured service, as it will require significant changes to application design, with accompanying human capital skill building. In addition, the attempt by application groups to reduce their costs by minimising use will affect Cloud providers, whether internal or public, as they will be forced to devise strategies to raise utilisation levels, so as to ensure their fixed costs are covered by the measured service charges they present.

Summary of Cloud Computing characteristics

In summary, these are the five Cloud Computing characteristics that comprise the NIST definition:

- *On-demand self-service* Provisioning decisions are made by resource users, not resource providers. Users are typically provided a portal for resource provisioning and control the entire processes themselves. Represents a shift of power from infrastructure and operations to applications groups.
- *Broad network access* Applications can be accessed from anywhere by a wide variety of devices. No limitation to 'approved devices' or the like is acceptable. Commonly associated with the availability of API interfaces for external program access.
- *Resource pooling* All compute resources are aggregated into a pool, available for use by anyone approved for general access. Previous practices such as assigning specific resources to particular groups are discarded in favour of general pooling, thereby making it easier for applications to obtain required resources.
- *Rapid elasticity* Resources may be assigned from the resource pool dynamically and quickly. Measures to make it easy for applications to grow and shrink are in place to ensure they can obtain sufficient resources in high load situations, while also being able to release resources back to the pool during lower load periods.
- *Measured service* Costs for computing resources are assigned on a highly granular basis, with some form of resource-use assignment tracked at the application level.

A move to direct resource chargeback is common, due to this characteristic.

As noted at the beginning of the Cloud Computing Characteristics section, this part of the NIST Cloud Computing definition is the most revolutionary part of the definition – despite the definition being couched in innocuous language with no particular emphasis being made about the radical implications contained within the definition. The downplaying of how profoundly Cloud Computing affects the future of IT is curious, and raises the question why NIST chose to present its description of Cloud Computing characteristics in such unobjectionable terms.

One explanation is that NIST is a governmental agency, and by their nature, governmental entities typically seek to avoid controversy. Besides the reticence associated with governmental entities, many parties have had a hand in crafting this definition, and such joint efforts commonly result in a bland end product.

Nevertheless, when one ponders the five characteristics and considers what they will really mean in action, it's obvious that Cloud Computing is deeply disruptive, with challenges presented to every group within IT and to every process used in the IT value chain.

Cloud Computing definition summary

As one can see from this review of the NIST Definition, Cloud Computing is a beguiling topic – seemingly straightforward, but, once delved into, challenging and full of unexpected implications.

Indeed, one of the most challenging aspects of Cloud Computing is how difficult it is for many people to comprehend how the marriage of virtualisation and automation transforms IT in unexpected ways. Too many view Cloud Computing as a minor and incremental improvement on existing practices; in fact, the most common shortcoming we see is that people fail to recognise how the logic of automation and self-service requires changing aspects of IT seemingly removed from servers and virtual machines.

To take one example, many people who embrace the more rapid provisioning associated with Cloud Computing fail to discern that full automation requires that governance and approval processes must be automated as well, which requires capturing these processes in rules, which can be implemented in automated policies.

We will return to this topic of how Cloud Computing changes established practices and processes in the next chapter, in which we will address how Cloud Computing changes IT security.

To close this chapter on Cloud Computing delineation, it is useful to turn back to the example that opened the chapter – *The New York Times* use of Cloud Computing for digital file translation – and examine how it illustrates the material presented in this chapter.

What *The New York Times* tells us about Cloud Computing

This single example illustrates both the promise of Cloud Computing and the challenge it poses to established IT processes and practices.

First, let's look at the benefits *The Times* achieved by using Cloud Computing:

- It increased business agility by leveraging Cloud Computing resources. This enabled the company to respond more rapidly to the changing business conditions it faced. Following established practices would have meant a delay of months while sufficient funding was obtained and equipment procured and installed.
- It was extremely cost-effective. Instead of the $100,000 plus that the traditional *Times* computing mode would have required, the engineer was able to complete the entire project at a small fraction of the traditional cost.
- It was efficient. No large project team was required to implement the solution. Because the engineer used AWS, no operations personnel or project managers were needed; no project task force to co-ordinate all the different groups involved in the project was necessary. A single engineer could take responsibility for the complete endeavour.
- The project aligned well with the self-service, pay-as-you-go model of Cloud Computing. It took only one weekend to complete the project. Once the project was finished, the engineer released the resources back to Amazon, which could make them available to another customer. Had the project been implemented in the traditional manner, *The Times* would have purchased 100 servers, to use them for only two days. They would have sat idle for the remainder of their useful life. Realistically, of course, this purchase would not have been made. Either *The Times* would not have made any investment for a project that would last but two days, or it would have made minimal resources available, which would have caused the project to take much longer to complete. This would have delayed project completion

and caused *The Times* to lose valuable time in pursuing its business goal.

On the other hand, using a Cloud Computing provider also presented the following challenges to *The Times*:

- No organisation oversight was exercised. While the project was efficiently implemented, the decisions of a single individual bypassed involvement by other groups. In this example, the outcome was very favourable; however, it is easy to envision other situations in which critical organisational input or review would be circumvented. Indeed, this so-called 'shadow IT', in which individuals or business units take advantage of Cloud Computing to avoid IT oversight, is renowned as a common phenomenon of Cloud Computing.

- Critical application components might be left out. While software necessary for the functionality of the application might be installed, it might also be possible that software components necessary for security, performance, application monitoring or the like could be deliberately or accidently omitted.

- Critical compliance requirements might not be met. It is unlikely that the format conversion project posed compliance issues for *The Times*, but it easy to imagine other projects that would have important compliance requirements that might not be addressed by a project of the type described. Many times, applications carry with them commitments regarding data privacy, location or management. Without involving people knowledgeable about the requirements of the individual project, important compliance measures might be omitted, thereby exposing the company to legal, financial or reputation risk.

- Application cost might overrun as a result of Cloud Computing pricing. Clearly, this project had a very attractive economic outcome: $240 versus $100,000 plus. However, Cloud Computing pricing is typically imposed on the basis of resource use. Another application that did not match the profile of the format conversion project could end up costing much more than an internal alternative.

In short, *The New York Times* case study is an excellent illustration of many aspects of Cloud Computing, both positive and potentially negative. Everything turned out well in this case study, but other projects might suffer from some of the shortcomings just outlined.

Certainly, the most commonly cited concern regarding Cloud Computing adoption is security. People are concerned about the security of applications placed in Cloud Computing environment and confused about what steps they should take to ensure proper security is implemented. To address those concerns and areas of confusion is the purpose of the remainder of this book.

CHAPTER 2: HOW CLOUD COMPUTING CHANGES SECURITY, GOVERNANCE, RISK AND COMPLIANCE

Survey after survey identifies security as people's number one concern about Cloud Computing. IT organisations decide to continue existing on-premises deployment practices (often using a private Cloud environment) because they have higher confidence in the security of their own environment.

But a curious thing emerges when one engages in a discussion on this topic. When IT professionals are asked what specific concerns about Cloud Computing security they have, responses like these are common:

- What's to prevent a Cloud service provider employee from sticking a thumb drive into a server and downloading my data?
- How do I know if my company's data is kept locally or stored in another country?
- What guarantees do I have about my application's uptime when it runs in a Cloud Computing environment?
- What financial compensation can I receive if my application is unavailable?
- How can I know if the Cloud service provider is applying appropriate patches to the hypervisor it uses to provide its Cloud Computing environment?
- How can my company govern who is able to manage resources in the Cloud Computing environment?

What's clear from these questions is that the word security is used to represent a range of concerns, only some of which focus on security, and others which focus on other areas that are associated with security, but are actually associated with other concerns.

For example, the topic of financial compensation in the event of downtime is not security related, but rather falls into the area of risk. The question regarding change management with respect to infrastructure resources in Cloud Computing environments relates to governance. And the question regarding hypervisor patching practices rests squarely in traditional security issues.

This conflating of concerns under the term security represents a significant challenge for those seeking to understand how to translate existing practices used for on-premises environments to the new world of Cloud Computing.

More troubling is what underpins these questions: the assumption that the responsibility for the area under discussion sits entirely with the Cloud service provider. The fact is that Cloud Computing represents a shared responsibility, with the demarcation line for where the responsibility is divided between the user and the Cloud provider varying according to the area and also according to what delivery mode is being evaluated.

One sometimes hears the demarcation line of responsibility referred to as a 'trust boundary', which illustrates that for those areas that fall into the Cloud provider's area of responsibility, users must trust the implementation and execution of the provider. There are techniques of evaluation, to be sure, which will be discussed in detail in this book, but at the end of the day, users must place trust in the provider as to its upholding of its responsibility.

As a starting point, it's appropriate to understand how the three different areas of security, compliance and risk interact in Cloud Computing. Even more important, it's important to understand how the responsibility for those is shared between the Cloud user and the Cloud provider. Two figures will be used to illustrate these questions.

Relationship between security, compliance and risk

To understand the interaction between security, compliance and risk, please refer to *Figure 1*. The figure represents how the three areas together form a whole. Significantly, both security and compliance indicate a boundary within those areas, with both the Cloud provider and Cloud user retaining responsibility for a portion of that area.

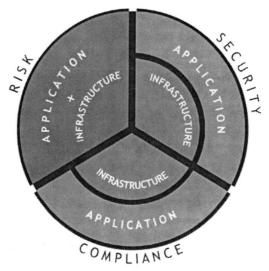

Figure 1: Security, risk and compliance

When it comes to risk, however, no such boundary exists. This lack of a boundary represents the fact that all service agreements shift primary responsibility for risk to the user. Should a Cloud application fail in availability, cause a financial loss to the Cloud user, or even fail to comply with important compliance requirements, the Cloud provider limits its responsibility significantly, typically to a refund of fees.

This asymmetric risk arrangement may seem unfair – after all, the Cloud provider's decisions and operations may cause a failure in compliance, which results in a financial penalty (i.e. a risk outcome borne by the Cloud user). So why should the financial responsibility be applied to the Cloud user instead of the Cloud provider which caused the compliance failure?

Despite this perception of unfairness, this careful assignment of risk responsibility to the Cloud user is universal throughout the Cloud Computing world. Individual Cloud providers may have slight differences among what they will provide in compensation for service failures; for example, one provider may offer a credit for service unavailability on a one-to-one basis (i.e. if the service is down for one hour, the Cloud user will receive one hour's credit to the monthly service cost), while another will refund a week's service costs for an outage of one hour. Despite these differences, though, every provider limits its financial exposure to service unavailability.

It's important to understand that this risk limitation is not unique to Cloud Computing. Outsource providers (e.g. firms that take over operating a company's IT data centre) also limit their financial responsibility in the event of an outage. Therefore, it is important not to regard this risk limitation as a complete restriction on using a Cloud provider, unless, that is, a company regards any risk limitation by a service provider as unacceptable. In that case, the company should continue to operate its own computing environment and forego use of an external Cloud provider.

The important point from this discussion is that when Cloud Computing security is raised as an issue, other issues are often being addressed. It's important to distinguish what type of issue is of concern, as that will change the method of evaluating the issue, the demarcation of the trust boundary and the appropriate actions to be taken by the Cloud user.

To help distinguish which issue is being evaluated and how to identify the trust boundary appropriate for the issue, *Figure 1* can be used as an aid.

Understanding the trust boundary

As noted, in the areas of compliance and security, the Cloud user and Cloud provider both hold some of the responsibility. The interface between where one party's responsibility ends and the other begins may be referred to as the trust boundary.

While the existence of a trust boundary intuitively makes sense, two questions arise:

- How can a Cloud user know where the trust boundary lies? After all, the service of a SaaS provider is quite different from that of an IaaS provider. So how can one know where the boundary lies?

- Once the boundary is defined, what can the Cloud user do to verify that the Cloud provider is adhering to its responsibility? In other words, what are the appropriate actions to take to ensure the Cloud provider lives up to its commitments?

One might ask, what does the trust boundary represent? In its basic form, the trust boundary represents a demarcation line: on one side of the line, the Cloud provider possesses responsibility for security measures; on the other, the Cloud user possesses responsibility.

For example, in an IaaS environment, it is clear that the Cloud provider has responsibility for physical security of the computing facility. It is also clear that the Cloud user is responsible for the application code.

On the Cloud provider's side, it is in control of what security practices are followed; the Cloud user can only audit what information about those practices the Cloud provider offers and evaluate whether the practices are sufficient for the user's needs. On the user's side of the trust boundary, the Cloud user can determine what the correct security practices are and can take active steps to implement those practices.

In short, on the Cloud provider's side of the trust boundary, the user is a passive assessor of what the Cloud provider implements in terms of security practices. On the Cloud user's side of the trust boundary, the user is an active implementer of security practices.

As you've probably guessed, the location of the trust boundary varies according to what model of Cloud Computing is being used: IaaS, PaaS or SaaS. Each model has the Cloud provider taking on differing levels of responsibility for the total application, and thereby affects where the trust boundary is located.

To help you better understand the trust boundary of the various models, and provide guidance as to how you should approach ensuring security for your Cloud applications, please see *Figure 2*.

Figure 2 is a chart of security responsibilities of each of the three Cloud delivery models, along three key areas of responsibility: infrastructure, operating system and middleware, and application.

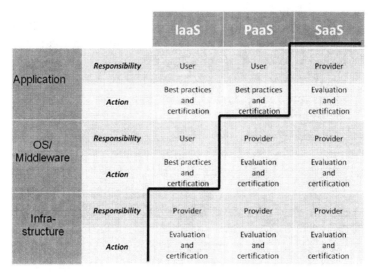

		IaaS	PaaS	SaaS
Application	*Responsibility*	User	User	Provider
	Action	Best practices and certification	Best practices and certification	Evaluation and certification
OS/ Middleware	*Responsibility*	User	Provider	Provider
	Action	Best practices and certification	Evaluation and certification	Evaluation and certification
Infra- structure	*Responsibility*	Provider	Provider	Provider
	Action	Evaluation and certification	Evaluation and certification	Evaluation and certification

Figure 2: Cloud security responsibilities

Here are brief descriptions of each area of responsibility:

- *Infrastructure* This area addresses both physical security and software security. Physical security refers both to the physical infrastructure of the Cloud Computing environment (i.e. the data centre itself) and the security practices surrounding the physical infrastructure. For example, this area covers whether the data centre has redundant Internet access methods, as well as what practices are in place regarding access to the physical facility (e.g. requiring both identification documents and biometric scanning as prerequisites for entering the data centre facility). Physical infrastructure would also refer to the hardware within the data centre like back-up generators and so on. Finally, infrastructure also refers to the software infrastructure used to implement the Cloud Computing environment. Most Cloud Computing (though not all) uses virtualisation as a foundation for the Cloud Computing environment, so this security area would cover the virtualisation hypervisor, including security practices related to controlling access to logging in to administer the virtualisation and ensuring proper security patches are installed.

- *Operating system and middleware* This area refers to software components that provide the operating environment within which the application runs. Key security issues for this area of responsibility include whether appropriate security software is installed within the OS, patch installation practices, administrative access to manage these components, and so on.
- *Application* This area refers to the software used to provide the actual functionality of the application itself. Falling under this area are topics like: software component version verification, patch installation practices, application identity management, and the like.

In *Figure 2*, you will see a thick black zigzag line. This indicates where the trust boundary lies for each Cloud delivery model. As an example, in a PaaS environment, the

Cloud provider is responsible for the security of the infrastructure and the middleware, while the Cloud user retains responsibility for the security of the application itself. As you can see from the descriptions, this means that the Cloud user would need to audit and evaluate whether the security measures of the provider in its areas of responsibility are sufficient.

In the next chapter, we'll review exactly what tools and aids Cloud users can leverage for both security approaches: audit/evaluation and implementation. For now, it's important to recognise that Cloud security measures are a shared responsibility and that, depending upon the Cloud delivery model, there is a trust boundary between the Cloud provider and the Cloud user.

There is one final point to be made about the trust boundary. Every Cloud provider offers a security framework into which users integrate their application. Naturally, every provider has a somewhat different framework, so it's incumbent upon users to understand the framework and ensure that they integrate with it properly. In fact, it's more than crucial. Without understanding the security framework presented by the Cloud provider, it's likely that the Cloud user will fail to configure its usage properly, and thereby leave security vulnerabilities that may be exploited by attackers.

Governance, compliance and risk in a Cloud environment

A cliché of the military is that generals always prepare to fight the last war, and are unprepared for the next war, which incorporates new developments in military technology and techniques.

One might make the same observation about computing governance, compliance and risk. Each of these suffers from operating in the ultra-dynamic field of computing, in which the relentless march of Moore's Law very quickly changes the way computing is done.

To take the example at hand, Cloud Computing with its self-service and elastic provisioning leverages automation to obviate manual system administration and shrink deployment times from weeks to minutes. However, most governance and compliance practices were designed for the old, slow-moving provisioning practices of a decade ago. These practices are now changing rapidly and causing problems for organisations trying to manage governance and compliance. These organisations are trying to manage incredibly fast operational practices with ponderous manual governance practices no longer capable of keeping up.

This confrontation between lightning-fast operations and human-speed management practices presents an impedance mismatch: simply put, the capability of the technology is in conflict with the capability of the organisation.

Some of the ways this mismatch plays out:

- *Data storage location* Many nations impose strict requirements on where personal information may be stored. Most require that personal information of their citizens be stored within the borders of the country. However, Cloud providers may serve customers of many nations from a single location, making those customers non-compliant with these laws. Even worse, a Cloud provider might migrate the data from one location to another, causing a previously compliant situation to go out of compliance – without the customer even being aware of the shift.

- *Storage privacy* Along with storage location, many nations (and, indeed, sub-national governmental entities like states, cities and regulatory bodies) impose requirements as to managing the privacy of personal information. Requirements for data encryption are common, along with requirements associated with notification in the event of a data breach. Many Cloud providers expect their customers to understand these requirements and ensure that they may be satisfied – even though the customer may not be able to control critical configuration parameters or operational practices.

- *Process challenges* In an effort to improve quality, many IT organisations have adopted standardised processes. ITIL® is the leading example of this. By implementing standardised processes, IT organisations reduce mistakes, ensure consistent practices and improve quality measures like application uptime and system performance. Unfortunately, many of these process definitions were created in a world of slow-moving manual processes, and assume that time is available for committee meetings, review groups and manual approval workflows. These process definitions are ill-suited for the rapid, automated provisioning practices of Cloud Computing.

It is important not to be too downcast when pondering these governance and compliance risks. The speedy evolution of computing has gone on for many years and challenged existing governance and compliance measures for just as long. The groups associated with assessing these topics are now examining how governance and compliance measures must be modified in light of Cloud Computing and they will eventually issue updated requirements, so that IT organisations can stay compliant. In the meantime, however, IT organisations will have to take on more responsibility for evaluating how to manage governance and compliance.

Security in a Cloud Computing environment

Now that we've addressed the types of issues associated with governance and compliance in Cloud Computing environments, let's dive into understanding the security issues associated with Cloud Computing. In other words, what are the security issues raised by operating in a Cloud Computing environment, and what security differences exist for users between their existing on-premises non-Cloud environments and their Cloud Computing environments?

The challenge of dynamism

Many security practices of the past were predicated on the assumption of a physical, static computing environment. Security practices were often applied as part of a review process as an application was put into production, which is to say, they were applied retrospectively, after application development.

Security practices also assumed an environment that didn't change very much. Once an application was put into production, its deployment topology wouldn't change much. If it had three servers at the web tier, it could be assumed that it would always have three servers, and any changes to the topology would be part of a deliberate change management process that would allow for review by security to ensure appropriate measures were put into place.

Finally, security practices (and most security products) assumed a physical computing world – in other words applications ran on physical servers, and the focus of security practices could be aimed at individual servers.

Cloud Computing changes all of that.

First of all, Cloud Computing leverages virtualisation, which breaks the association between application and physical server. Virtualisation means that each application runs in its own virtual machine, which may migrate from one server to another. So assuming security can be tied to physical resources is no longer practical.

Cloud Computing extends virtualisation to add dynamism – the ability for applications to rapidly change deployment topology. Moreover, user self-service (NIST Cloud Computing characteristic Number One) means that the assumptions of extended deployment timelines, with sufficient opportunity for security review and implementation prior to moving an application into production, are no longer appropriate.

The challenge of a shared environment

The move away from dedicated physical resources into a virtualised Cloud environment also means that applications now operate in a shared environment – a pool of computing resources shared among all users (NIST Cloud Computing characteristic Number Three). In essence, this means that no single user 'owns' the environment. It also means that many security practices that are appropriate for a dedicated environment are not acceptable in a Cloud Computing one.

What does this imply?

Many organisations protect themselves against malicious traffic by placing a traffic monitoring device (i.e. a security appliance) on the data centre network. All network traffic is passed through that device to identify and prevent outside intrusions.

In a pooled resource environment, no user controls the infrastructure, so the common appliance solution is not possible – after all, one user's traffic examination appliance is another user's intrusion threat. Consequently, the shared environment of Cloud Computing negates many traditional security practices.

The challenge of security deperimeterisation

You may be unfamiliar with the phrase 'deperimeterisation of security'. It was coined by a security consortium called the Jericho Forum, part of the Open Group. The basic concept can be summed up as recognising that the traditional model of security based on hardening the perimeter between computers and the outside world is no longer appropriate in a world in which applications are routinely opened up for access by external partners and customers. Blocking access into the data centre by all but company employees would obviate the purpose for many applications.

Furthermore, attempting to impose the old hardened perimeter model will simply invite insecure computing environments as companies bypass existing security practices in furtherance of the goal of collaborating with business partners without replacing those practices without something more appropriate.

Key to responding to this deperimeterisation of security is recognising that security must be placed at the endpoint, ensuring that every part of an application is protected.

Cloud security challenges summary

Cloud Computing marries virtualisation and automation and requires changing established operating practices. With respect to security, the shortened timeframes between deployment decision and computing operations means that leisurely review processes and lengthy after-the-fact security implementations are no longer workable.

Security in a Cloud Computing world must support:

- dynamic infrastructures
- operating in a shared, pooled infrastructure
- protection in a deperimeterised environment.

The traditional models of computing security were challenged well before Cloud Computing, but face even greater issues with the advent of the Cloud.

Conclusion

Cloud Computing is a combination of virtualisation, process automation and dynamic response to changing application conditions. None of these, on its own, is anything more than a logical extension of existing IT conditions; the combination, however, changes the way IT operates.

In this chapter, we examined several changes associated with Cloud Computing:

- *Dynamism* The rapid provisioning of computing resources, as well as rapid change in application topologies as computing resources are dynamically added and subtracted in response to changing application load.

- *Pooled resources* Cloud Computing abstracts use from assets, where use (i.e. application operation) is not associated with a particular set of computing resources, but instead is hosted in a general pool of computing resources. This means that the location of specific application components may change from time to time as loads are rebalanced within the resource pool. It also means that security measures must not be associated with specific hardware, but must instead migrate dynamically along with the application as it moves from one set of computing resources to another.

- *Security deperimeterisation* Because Cloud applications operate in a dynamic, shared resource pool, traditional security solutions are often unusable. Relying on a network-attached appliance to examine all network traffic is unworkable, due to restrictions imposed by Cloud providers. Moreover, the ongoing opening up of applications to external parties like partners and customers also means that the traditional model of imposing strong security at the data centre perimeter (i.e. relying on a restrictive firewall to prevent traffic from reaching internal resources) is unsustainable as well. The new model of security requires that each endpoint implements security measures to protect itself as appropriate.

These changes, combined, mean that the traditional models of security, governance and compliance all change in the world of Cloud Computing.

CHAPTER 3: GOVERNANCE OF CLOUD COMPUTING

Governance: a: to control, direct or strongly influence the actions and conduct of. (*www.webster.com*)

Given the vast changes (economic, technological, geopolitical) that businesses and governments need to react to, managing risk has become a key initiative for many organisations. Governance is one tool that can be used to minimise risk by providing consistent controls and processes regarding the management of assets.

The topic of governance is rapidly gaining support within the enterprise IT community. Typically the nature of information technology within mid-sized and large enterprises forces the need to implement some form of governance, albeit usually on a case-by-case basis. Only with regard to certain systems and applications is governance now becoming a respected first-class enterprise effort backed by executive management. This change in attitude is being fostered by the rapidly changing IT landscape and a realisation by executive management that they are not properly positioned to take advantage of emerging technology trends that could potentially lead to expense reduction and cost savings or provide much needed agility.

IT governance is a system of ensuring that IT assets are provided the appropriate levels of supervision, monitoring and control relative to its role in effecting the mission or strategic goals of the organisation. Hence, anything that views, touches, changes, or in any way impacts the quality, authenticity or availability of the data or applications, requires some level of governance. Moreover, the amount and type of governance applied should be relative in cost and effort to the importance of that data or application to the mission of the business, as is true of any risk-management endeavour.

An IT governance programme should address the following types of questions:

- Who decides if a particular IT programme is meeting the needs and goals of the business?
- Who decides how IT funds will be allocated and apportioned?
- Who decides to implement a change in function or capability of a system?
- Who decides which resources have access to a particular subset of data?
- Who decides what data will be stored and where it will be stored?
- Who defines policies related to data, application and service usage for the business?

Note that these questions have nothing to do with the technology aspects of IT, but instead they focus on the management of IT or IT service management. This is a great entry point to start the discussion of IT governance and Cloud Computing. Businesses have been outsourcing IT functions for many years. In some cases, the business leaders have put little thought behind the long-term implications to the business while focusing solely on costs. In other cases, very expensive legal agreements have been cast with regard to the outsourcing that covers every imaginable outcome. Both are extremes that require the practice of governance to bring balance.

From the perspective of outsourcing, Cloud Computing is not a brand new construct based on no prior experience. Cloud Computing does, however, introduce nuances for IT governance insomuch as adoption of these services are no longer being introduced into the organisation solely by the IT department. Moreover, the expectation by users that Cloud provides the ability to consume resources in an uncontrolled and unbounded manner can result in negative impact to the business. Governance is required to ensure that the value of Cloud is recognised, but that expectations are appropriately set and managed.

Which governance framework is right for Cloud?

There are multiple governance frameworks that can be applied to governance of information technology. Some of these have overlapping concerns and in some cases it takes more than one to ensure adherence to regulations and standards. Here's a short list of the more popular frameworks just to illustrate the point:

- Information Technology Infrastructure Library (ITIL)
- ISO/IEC 38500
- SOA Governance
- Enterprise Architecture
- Control OBjectives for Information and related Technology (COBIT) ®
- Capability Maturity Model (CMM) ®
- Sarbanes-Oxley
- Health Insurance Portability and Accountability Act (HIPAA)
- Basel II
- ISO/IEC 20000.

Some of the items in this list focus on corporate governance, while others focus on financial, operational or data governance. Organisations will use a combination of these depending upon the community they service and the corporate structure under which they operate.

For purposes of this book, we are going to focus on four governance frameworks that are used to minimise risk with regard to Cloud Computing:

- ITIL
- Enterprise Architecture
- SOA Governance
- ISO/IEC 20000.

Cloud Computing touches so many aspects of IT that choosing which governance frameworks to adhere to can be a difficult task. Most organisations will most likely use the governance framework they are already using for IT, which in many cases is ITIL version 2 or 3 – a recognised worldwide standard that offers certification. ITIL is a fine framework for implementing IT service management, but its lack of detail for how to implement certain aspects of the framework can prove challenging for some organisations.

ITIL v3 is the third iteration of the ITIL framework and focuses heavily on IT Service Management (ITSM) or delivering IT as a service. As you can see this aligns well with Cloud Computing, since Cloud Computing focuses on delivery of compute resources as a service. ITIL is divided up into sections or books with each book focusing on an aspect of service delivery. There are currently five books: Service Strategy, Service Design, Service Transition, Service Operation and Continual Service Improvement (*see Figure 3*).

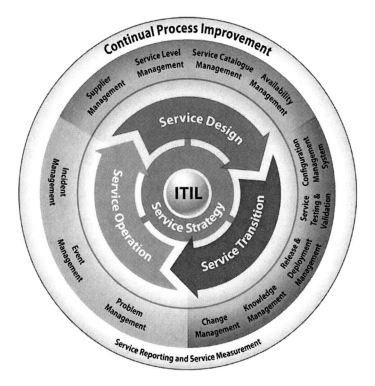

Figure 3: ITIL v3

The goal of ITIL v3 is to provide a framework for analysing and prioritising the needs of the business and delivering the appropriate services with the required capabilities. Moreover, the framework is designed to consistently review past assumptions and requirements in light of the ever-changing business landscape and continually improve the overall service catalogue in an attempt to provide a high level of quality in IT. We will further explore this concept of quality in IT later in the chapter.

Enterprise Architecture (EA) is not a governance framework in the traditional sense, but it definitely provides guidance to the business with regard to managing technology adoption. EA and ITIL are not mutually exclusive. Indeed, ITIL v3 tends to focus on operational concerns whereas EA take a much more holistic view of the IT environment. Additionally, since Cloud Computing is defined as a service architecture, some may find EA frameworks offer a bit more structure than ITIL v3.

Examples of EA frameworks that can be used to govern the use of Cloud Computing include: The Open Group Architecture Framework (TOGAF), Federal Enterprise Architecture (FEA), Zachman Framework and the Department of Defense Architecture Framework (DoDAF). Each of these frameworks is designed to assist enterprises in managing complexity and increased rate of change. They allow organisations to model how business strategy will be satisfied by business processes and corresponding systems. Hence, Cloud Computing should be a consideration within multiple levels of your Enterprise Architecture.

In contrast to ITIL, EA does not focus on the detailed processes associated with governance. However, without EA, it will be difficult for an organisation to have an understanding of how all the pieces fit together and impact the other pieces. For example, how can an organisation fully understand the implications for governing a single service, if they do not have a broad understanding of the following?

- Who are the users of a service?
- What services is this service dependent on?
- What data does this service operate on and who is the owner of that data?

- What business processes are affected by this service?
- What business processes use this service?

Enterprise Architecture, in tandem with other governance frameworks, enables a well-rounded approach to IT governance. EA is useful when adopting Cloud Computing because it will allow the organisation to understand the impact of moving aspects of governance to the Cloud service provider, migrating silos into multi-tenant environments and identifying the changes required in business processes to support the use of Cloud Computing.

Organisations that are not building their own Clouds or acting as Cloud service providers may also consider using Service Oriented Architecture (SOA) governance since SOA is focused on the delivery of software services to users. SOA governance refers to the organisation structure, processes, policies and standards specifically focused on the life cycle of services, metadata and composite applications in a service-oriented architecture. SOA governance is an extension of IT governance, which helps to ensure that the concepts and principles for service orientation and its architecture are managed appropriately and are in alignment with the goals of the business.

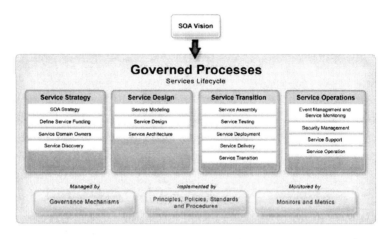

Figure 4: Service Oriented Architecture governance

As illustrated by *Figure 4*, SOA governance models aspects of the ITIL v3 framework extending it into development of service-oriented systems, whereas ITIL v3 focuses on all aspects of IT management.

Given that for some the Cloud represents an application-centric operations model (GigaOm, 2011)[1] – that is the Cloud is focused on delivery of applications to users without the overhead of managing the infrastructure, such as with Platform-as-a-Service – SOA governance may be a more appropriate governance model. SOA governance removes all the governance overhead associated with data centre operations and infrastructure security controls that have no implications for Cloud users, leaving a more nimble and agile approach to governance.

---

[1] *http://gigaom.com/cloud/what-cloud-boils-down-to-for-the-enterprise-2/#comment-682274*

The International Organisation for Standardization's ISO/IEC 20000 was developed in 2005 by ISO/IEC JTC1 SC7 (Software and systems engineering subcommittee) and revised in 2011. The ISO/IEC 20000 is divided into two parts:

- Part 1 – promotes the adoption of an integrated process approach to effectively deliver managed services to meet the business and customer requirements.
- Part 2 – describes the best practices for service management within the scope of ISO/IEC 20000-1.

These two parts are focused on the following categories:

- scope
- terms and definitions
- planning and implementing service management
- requirements for a management system
- planning and implementing new or changed services
- service delivery processes
- relationship processes
- control processes
- resolution processes
- release process.

As represented on the ISO website, the ISO/IEC 20000-1 supports the following needs:

- an organisation seeking services from service providers and requiring assurance that their service requirements will be fulfilled;
- an organisation that requires a consistent approach by all its service providers, including those in a supply chain;

- a service provider that intends to demonstrate its capability for the design, transition, delivery and improvement of services that fulfil service requirements;
- a service provider to monitor, measure and review its service management processes and services;
- a service provider to improve the design, transition, delivery and improvement of services through the effective implementation and operation of the service management system (SMS);
- an assessor or auditor as the criteria for a conformity assessment of a service provider's SMS to the requirements in ISO/IEC 20000-1:2011.

As noted by this description, there are many common requirements for IT governance. ISO/IEC 20000, SOA Governance and ITIL v3 all have overlapping concerns. The key to using these frameworks is to map them to your organisation's needs and capabilities. Attempting to implement all aspects of any of these frameworks can be a daunting task that requires an investment that may outweigh the benefit. Governance is a risk management tool and should be implemented insofar as the risks are mitigated. In this case, the risk is Cloud adoption and Cloud use.

Role of the service catalogue

Regardless which governance framework your organisation decides to implement, a key component is the service catalogue. The service catalogue provides the central registry for all services being offered including those that are both human and digital. It should provide a description of the service, entitlements, service levels, costs and a means to request use of the service. Moreover, the organisation should assign at least one individual as the catalogue manager. These individuals will be responsible for managing the content and ensuring the information is correct.

Note that some in IT have come to associate the service catalogue with service discovery. This idea has been promoted through early SOA efforts for the purposes of publishing services akin to the online application store that have been designed to support mobile devices. This is not the purpose for the service catalogue as it is being represented here. Moreover, this viewpoint undermines the role of the service catalogue as defined by ITIL and ISO/IEC 20000, which is the core of these governance frameworks. Discovery is just one action that is supported by the service catalogue, but the more important role is to support the whole of the governance process.

Consider the following: an enterprise acquires geospatial software with an application programming interface (API) that is used to deliver an in-house developed geospatial service. The software company charges per user and the organisation has the responsibility to ensure that each request to the API is made by a legally registered user. Initially, there are only three users for the service, so managing this overhead is reasonable. After two years, the number of users for the service grows to 500, making API calls through three different applications.

To continue, the first application developed to use this service provided single sign-on and appropriately registered all users. However, the teams delivering the next two applications using the service were forced to deliver quickly and decided that they would make all requests through a single trusted user. Since there was no documentation that explained to developers the requirements for using the geospatial service, such as would be documented in the service catalogue, they had no reason to believe their actions would result in a legal impact to the organisation.

The moral of the story is that services get aggregated and develop dependencies. The service catalogue facilitates a full understanding of the usage and responsibilities of the consumer in consuming a service. It is a mission-critical piece of information pertaining to the running of your business and helps to ensure appropriate and legal usage, thus mitigating the potential of future legal risk.

If you consider an IT world where software licences share a 1:1 relationship with the physical equipment on which the software is deployed, then managing and tracking licences is a fairly straightforward activity. However, when you consider that a piece of software may be deployed on a virtual machine, which may be replicated in an automated fashion and of which hundreds of snapshots are made for purposes of recovery, then managing the use of that licence becomes a daunting task.

Cloud Computing governance begs for automated licence management. The best solution for enterprises would be automated registration of software into a global registry upon invocation. Thus, every time an instance of that software is invoked, the identifier of the machine it's running on would be captured enabling a complete and accurate count of the number of licences in use within the enterprise. An even simpler solution, albeit more expensive and perhaps wasteful based on actual usage, would be an enterprise licence that removes the need to track usage on an individual basis.

Further complicating this endeavour is that software companies are struggling with the appropriate model for pricing the use of their software. Pricing models vary from per machine pricing to number of CPU cores to number of users. These approaches to pricing all suffer from various problems, but ultimately, the onus is on the organisation to track and understand their own usage. The vendor always reserves the right to audit usage to ensure the customer has not exceeded the agreed-upon usage for the software. Cloud Computing makes this requirement murkier and more ambiguous, thus raising enterprise risk without either party fully understanding the ramifications. The service catalogue is key for setting the policy based upon the vendor agreement and then assisting with enforcement through governance, risk and compliance (GRC) tools.

Dude, where's my server? (The need for policy management)

Another major consideration related to governance of Cloud Computing is policy management, specifically regarding location of the allocated resources. A Cloud service provider – this includes internal IT as a service provider on a private Cloud – must drive for maximum utilisation of compute resources in order to fully gain the financial benefits of Cloud Computing. If a Cloud service provider does not actively reconfigure the runtime environment to utilise resources effectively, they will need to spend additional funds to acquire more compute resources to satisfy demand.

Anyone who has used a PC running a version of either DOS or Windows® can relate to the following analogy to the utilisation problem. A brand new system writes all the files to the hard disk in a contiguous manner, but over time as these files get re-written and extended, they begin to get fragmented across the disk. Fragmentation results in more latency for reading, since the hard disk must seek to a new position before it can read the next block. To improve performance, Microsoft and other third-party vendors provided tools to defragment the disk.

A Cloud architecture suffers from similar fragmentation. As new instances of machines on IaaS and processes on PaaS start to claim memory, network and CPU, it begins to impact neighbouring machines/processes. So, a Cloud manager satisfying requests to allocate resources on a first-come, first-served basis may need to leave certain resources on a physical server unused because it cannot satisfy a new request and instead allocates those resources on a different server. Over time, the Cloud manager will need to reshuffle allocations across servers to optimise its physical resources or run the risk of not satisfying a request even though there's excess unused capacity.

The result of the need to defragment means that the Cloud service provider has limits to what they can promise with regards to where your machine/process is running. Perhaps they can promise that it will only run in certain data centres or on certain racks within data centres. However, eventually there is a good chance that the neighbours you had yesterday may not be the neighbours you have tomorrow. This has many performance and security implications for your Cloud application that will be discussed elsewhere in this book, but it also illustrates a need for governance and policy management with regard to Cloud management.

The double-edged sword for Cloud service providers is that users need the ability to specify and apply policies regarding:

- where resources can be allocated from in order to satisfy a request;
- what type of quality of service is required in order to operate effectively in the Cloud;
- under what conditions the machine/process can be migrated.

But, these are just the policies that are used by the Cloud manager. In addition to these, there are policies for security, access control, compliance, reporting, naming, sizing, quality-of-service, and so on. A strong Cloud governance strategy addresses all known policy constraints.

In the end, all of this directly relates to Service Level Management (SLM). In terms of ITIL, SLM is about managing the balance between quality of IT and the related costs. A utopian IT environment can spend infinitely on hardware, software, bandwidth and labour. Without constraint, the quality of IT should be extremely high. When the constraints of costs are applied, IT leadership must prioritise their efforts and focus to meet their mission objectives and ensure the greatest possible level of service.

Unfortunately, many end-users do not believe that their IT leadership is doing an effective job based on their own experiences, but what they don't fully understand is how much of the IT budget is spent on 'keeping the lights on'. That is, just maintaining the current level of IT quality typically consumes 55–65% of annual IT (Dignan, 2010)[2]. This leaves little funding for efforts that would increase overall IT quality.

Cloud Computing offers many technical advantages, but it is in this economic reality that Cloud Computing offers its greatest value. It enables a cost-effective means of attacking and reducing the current operational burden for businesses. Over time, this will mean that less money is being spent on the status quo and more is being spent to improve the overall quality of IT.

Conclusion

Adopting Cloud Computing without some form of governance will make it problematic to incorporate into formal IT processes later. One lesson we have learned over the years is that it's more difficult to put the genie back in the bottle than to let it out at all. Applying a governance framework even in a nominal manner will foster an ability to expand the types of controls applied as Cloud Computing becomes more ingrained in IT.

Businesses should focus on developing and managing their service catalogues effectively as part of their Cloud Computing strategy. The service catalogue will provide a wealth of knowledge about the operating environment, as well as provide a foundation for reporting and auditing. The

---

[2] Technology budgets 2010: Maintenance gobbles up software spending; SMBs shun Cloud.
http://www.zdnet.com/blog/btl/technology-budgets-2010-maintenance-gobbles-up-software-spending-smbs-shun-cloud/30873

service catalogue can greatly reduce possible legal risks from improper or invalid use of software.

Optimal Cloud Computing utilisation requires constant defragmentation. This means that the Cloud service provider needs the ability to migrate virtual machines and processes as part of the defragmentation process. The only way to mitigate potentially dangerous scenarios is if the Cloud service providers allow users to place constraints on when and how their machines/processes can be migrated. Thus, there must be a collaborative relationship between the Cloud service provider and the Cloud service consumer, or one will be at risk.

Additional resources

www.itsmfi.org

www.zifa.com

http://en.wikipedia.org/wiki/Service-oriented_architecture

www.iso.org

CHAPTER 4: CLOUD COMPUTING TOP SECURITY RISKS

In *Chapter 2*, we examined how Cloud Computing changes security, governance, risk and compliance. Building on that, in this chapter we will focus on the top security risks facing users of Cloud Computing.

Security – the shift from static to dynamic

Underlying every aspect of Cloud Computing security is the fact that the fundamental assumptions regarding the operating environment to which security practices are applied are different in the world of Cloud Computing.

In the past, security practices assumed the following:

- *Static and 'owned' computing environment* Security practices assumed that the foundations of computing environments – the data centre, physical infrastructure (electrical system, UPS, cooling, etc.), and so on – are under the direct control of the organisation the security group is associated with.
- *Operational practices performed by organisation employees* All changes to any part of the computing environment – from physical plant to application configurations – are performed by company employees or company-directed contractors. Those individuals answer to the company and have only its objectives guiding their actions.
- *Rarely changed application configurations and topology* Applications are difficult to install and configuring the components used by applications requires manual

interaction; therefore, it is hard to get things correct, and once they are implemented, they are modified as infrequently as possible. Best practices impose methodical planning and management oversight for proposed changes. No on-the-fly changes are supported or allowed.

- *Lengthy application projects and occasional application changes* The most common application project methodology is the waterfall method, in which projects go through distinct phases serially. Each phase's conclusion is marked by a milestone handoff. Because of the overhead of co-ordination, phases are typically of long duration and many changes are introduced at the infrequent project milestones. This commonly results in large code integration efforts and difficult handoffs at milestones due to introduced complexity.

Security practices in this environment align with its assumptions. This makes sense. In a rarely changing, wholly owned environment, security practices conform to project management practices for convenience and simplicity reasons.

This means that it makes sense to centralise security components; for example, intrusion detection and prevention measures may be installed in an appliance that sits on the data centre network and monitors traffic to all systems and applications. This allows security to be handled in one place and offers the opportunity to have specialists focus on a single device, rather than have every project team attempt to implement security for its environment.

These security practices also imply that application security practices can align with project timelines, being infrequently evaluated, manually reviewed via meetings or electronic documents, with recommendations manually applied by application or operations groups as part of their milestone commitments.

In summary, in static, rarely changing computing environments, it is appropriate for security practices to align with and reinforce the prevailing processes and practices.

Breakdown of security assumptions

However, computing environments have been evolving over the past decade and many of these assumptions are challenged by the changes in company IT practices.

Regarding deployment in outsourcing and hosting environments, many companies have outsourced their data centre operations to third parties. In some cases, this means that the third party takes over a company's data centre and continues operations. In other cases, though, the company's applications (and perhaps servers) are transferred to the third party's data centre. In the latter case, the practice of placing an appliance to host the company's security systems is probably not appropriate, given that the facility is shared with other users. Even if the third party uses an appliance approach, it will not be under the company's control and, therefore, direct configuration is not possible. In hosting environments, the assumption of complete control is further challenged, in that the hosting provider controls all infrastructure and the company has no control of anything other than application code and application component configuration.

As you will recall, we identified three key issues that challenge established security practices:

- *Dynamic infrastructure* In a Cloud Computing environment, applications commonly, and rapidly, change their topologies. Application components may shift from one server to another. Moreover, Cloud applications may add or subtract computing resources in response to application load. This dynamism challenges security practices designed for static environments.
- *Shared resources* In the past, servers were typically dedicated to specific applications, and collections of servers were often owned by specific company units (e.g. 'Those are the HR department's servers'). Cloud Computing, by contrast, treats the entire collection of computing resources as a resource pool to be shared among all applications. In public Cloud Computing environments, security practices that assumed ownership of an entire infrastructure and used appliances to implement security are not allowed.
- *Deperimeterisation of computing environments* Many organisations have focused security efforts by protecting the perimeter via strict firewall rules and refusing non-company traffic. The shift in business practices to closely working with partners and customers has meant that outside personnel are also accessing company applications, thereby requiring a more porous perimeter.

At the bottom of these changes is the fact that Cloud Computing is a new operating model based on virtualisation and operations automation. As such, it breaks the 'one application, one server' practices of the past and also accelerates deployment and shifting of computing resources.

Use of a public Cloud service provider further complicates this environment, as it introduces the need for a shared responsibility for security, with a trust boundary serving as the interface where the Cloud provider and Cloud user engage.

Taken together, these changes and the shared responsibility of Cloud service provider (CSP) environments raise a new set of challenges to security.

How should we characterise these challenges?

First, let's take a look at the implications of the trust boundary. After all, the trust boundary implies different actions on the part of a Cloud user. On the Cloud user's side of the trust boundary, the user will need to take active steps to address its responsibility. On the Cloud provider's side of the trust boundary, the user needs to assess whether the provider's security measure are sufficient.

We examined the trust boundary in *Chapter 2* via a figure reproduced again here as *Figure 5*. The table has a thick zigzag line that indicates how the trust boundary varies according to whether the Cloud delivery model is IaaS, PaaS or SaaS.

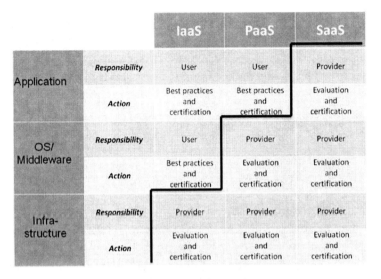

		IaaS	PaaS	SaaS
Application	*Responsibility*	User	User	Provider
	Action	Best practices and certification	Best practices and certification	Evaluation and certification
OS/ Middleware	*Responsibility*	User	Provider	Provider
	Action	Best practices and certification	Evaluation and certification	Evaluation and certification
Infra-structure	*Responsibility*	Provider	Provider	Provider
	Action	Evaluation and certification	Evaluation and certification	Evaluation and certification

Figure 5: Trust boundary

Focusing on the IaaS portion of the diagram, let's drill down into this topic and examine the trust boundary in more detail. In *Figure 6*, one can see a diagram containing all major elements that are required to deliver application functionality. The figure includes the computing facility, the internal data centre infrastructure (i.e. those components necessary to operate the facility, like fire suppression and UPS), the hardware infrastructure and network, and then the components of individual servers: computer, hypervisor, operating system, middleware and application software. At the top of the figure is the perimeter of the facility, depicted as the firewall, which represents all measures to filter traffic from the Internet and ensure that applications only receive appropriate network traffic.

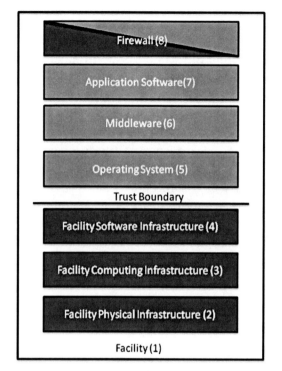

Figure 6: Elements to deliver application functionality

By looking at this diagram, one can see that there are many security elements present in a Cloud Computing environment. These elements comprise:

- those delivered by the Cloud service provider, which maintains responsibility for the element;
- those delivered by the user, who is responsible for their implementation and management;
- those delivered by the Cloud service provider but configured by the user. For example, many Cloud providers present a firewall to each user account to manage traffic in and out of the applications installed by

the user, who is responsible for ensuring that the firewall passes only appropriate traffic into virtual machine instances within the account's environment. This class of elements can be the most challenging for users to understand, as many users will assume that correct operations of the element (e.g. firewall) is the responsibility of the Cloud provider, failing to recognise that it is the user's responsibility to ensure the element operates properly. Continuing the firewall example, many users will assume the Cloud provider must make the firewall operate properly, since the provider delivers the firewall, rather than recognising that configuration (and responsibility for proper operation) must remain with the user – after all, how can the Cloud provider know what ports must be open for the user's application?

Let's examine the entire stack and assign security responsibility for each layer.

Facility: Cloud provider responsibility

The facility is the physical premises of the Cloud infrastructure and is always the responsibility of the Cloud provider. This entails ensuring that the facility is securely closed, with no possibility of entrance without being identified. Common practices for ensuring facility security include guards, who match personal identification with visual examination. Other measures used to control access to the facility may include biometric identification (e.g. retina scans), which are ordinarily used in addition to physical identification by a human guard. Perhaps the most extreme version of facility security is that practised by SuperNAP, which has ex-military armed guards on security duty.

Facility physical infrastructure: Cloud provider responsibility

Facility physical infrastructure refers to the mechanical devices that are housed within a facility and provide services necessary to operate a Cloud infrastructure. The reliability of these devices, along with management of these devices may have security implications. Common devices include:

- *Power input and distribution* Obviously, a reliable power supply is critical for running a data centre. Usually, a high-quality source of power with a good record of availability will be used to provide power to the facility. In addition within the facility, electricity will be distributed by power equipment. Increased investment in power distribution will allow more protection against power outages by use of redundant components.

- *Generators and uninterruptible power supplies* Despite the use of a reliable electricity supplier, sometimes power will be cut off. Data centres ordinarily have on-site protection against power losses. Most high-quality data centres have on-premises generators that can be used to supply power in the event of an electricity provider outage. In addition, most highly available data centres will have battery back-up to supply power for the period between electricity cut-off and the on-premises generators getting up to speed and delivering power.

- *Air conditioning and distribution* Servers throw off significant amounts of heat, and most data centres require air conditioning to keep temperatures within operating tolerances.

- *Infrastructure partitioning and security* Many Cloud data centres will have sections separated from one another for security purposes. Often these security mechanisms take the form of separate rooms or cages, each of which has its own access control. Another new form of partitioning is represented by the move to 'containerisation', which is a form of data centre deployment in which computing devices and racks (see next item in this list) are placed into a container. The container may be either an actual shipping container of the type used to ship goods throughout the world, or a custom-designed container that maintains the same general rectangular dimensions but is built to better support computing form factors by, say, allowing back-to-back racking. The advantage of containers is that they allow easier deployment as there is no need to construct an entire building; all that is needed is a level location to install the container. Some companies have even installed computing containers outside in secure parking lots.

- *Racks and/or cabinets*   Every data centre has some kind of physical structures that contain computing devices. These physical structures may be racks or cabinets (cabinets often have protective doors, while racks expose the computing devices). Perhaps somewhat surprisingly, significant change and innovation is going on in this area, with different form factors supporting better installation of blade or pizza-box servers, and some even supporting vertical installation of standard PC motherboards.

Facility computing infrastructure: Cloud provider responsibility

Facility computing infrastructure refers to the computing infrastructure necessary for the facility to operate as a data centre, but not associated with particular accounts or servers. In other words, this infrastructure is that necessary to serve the entire population of data centre users. This infrastructure includes:

- *External network and Internet connectivity* For high availability, Cloud infrastructure will ordinarily have two Internet connections, each from a different provider. In addition, good design practice dictates that each connection comes into the building from a different side, thereby precluding a single JCB excavator cutting both connections. Besides Internet connectivity, the facility may have additional network connections that provide direct, private connectivity between the facility and specific locations or customers. Both types of connectivity are crucial to provide highly available computing, which reduces risk.
- *Internal network infrastructure* Network traffic from individual computing devices runs across a shared network infrastructure. The performance and security of this shared infrastructure is the responsibility of the facility provider.
- *Storage devices* All storage within a Cloud provider's facility is shared, and responsibility for the storage infrastructure lies with the Cloud provider.

Computing hardware infrastructure: Cloud provider responsibility

Computing hardware infrastructure refers to the actual computing devices that operate in the data centre. If you remember the NIST definition referred to in an earlier chapter, these devices serve as a pooled resource, shared among all users, with application workloads migrated throughout the shared pool as necessary. This infrastructure includes:

- *Servers* These are the devices that perform computing; one may hear them referred to as performing processing. Ordinarily, in a Cloud Computing environment, a server supports a number of virtual machines, which are commonly being used by different users. Stated another way, servers are a shared resource used by whatever virtual machines the Cloud management software (see below) assigns to them. The Cloud provider is responsible for the servers in a Cloud environment.
- *Storage* Each virtual machine uses storage upon which it places its data. While the data is the responsibility of the user, the storage itself is the responsibility of the Cloud provider. This storage usually resides in the storage infrastructure, although some Cloud providers will use locally attached disk drives to store user data.
- *Network connectivity* Each server has one or more network interface cards that transmit and receive data to and from the network infrastructure.

Computing software infrastructure: Cloud provider responsibility

Computing software infrastructure refers to the software that is used to operate the Cloud Computing functionality that supports applications placed in the infrastructure. This infrastructure includes:

- *Hypervisors* Hypervisors are a software layer that resides between physical servers and the virtual machines running on those servers. Hypervisors form the basis of virtualisation, which in turn forms the basis of Cloud Computing. Responsibility includes initial installation, configuration, subsequent upgrades, installing patches, and perhaps code customisation.
- *Cloud orchestration software* As discussed previously, Cloud Computing represents virtualisation married to automation, which allows much faster provisioning times. Cloud Computing automation is accomplished via orchestration software, which translates a high-level command (e.g. create a new server instance) into the individual tasks necessary to accomplish that command (e.g. create new virtual machine, attach two terabytes of storage, assign a network address, etc.) and ensure they are accomplished as a single transaction. It is no exaggeration to say that orchestration represents the single most important operation in a working Cloud Computing environment.
- *API software* Cloud providers offer access to their services via service interfaces. While often referred to as API (application programming interface), these may not be a programming interface, but rather an online service that is accessed via the Internet using a common protocol like HTTP. For most Cloud providers, these online

interfaces are the foundation of interacting with their service and their availability and reliability are paramount in terms of keeping the service up and running.

- *Portal software* Most Cloud providers also offer an online browser interface that people use to interact with the functionality of the provider's Cloud infrastructure. This interface will have the ability to start, stop and suspend virtual machines, assign IP addresses to specific virtual machines, assign load balancers, and the like. The best practice for Cloud providers is that their portal software will use the service's API, becoming, in effect, an equal partner with all other programs accessing the service's functionality. While many users will choose to use an external tool to manage their Cloud resources (or indeed, will have their application directly interact with the CSP environment to obtain and release resources), many others will use the CSP's own portal offering.

- *System services* Many Cloud providers offer software components or services as part of the Cloud environment. For example, Amazon Web Services offers a message queue service for applications to use. These services can simplify application development, as the application creator does not need to take responsibility for these system services. Indeed, judicious leveraging of these services allows the application creator to focus on the unique functionality of the application and avoid effort devoted to lower-value plumbing.

- *Monitoring and management software* A CSP environment is a large and complex collection of computing resources – many servers, storage hardware, network devices, many software components, and so on

– that must be monitored to help ensure optimum uptime and performance.

- *Audit and staff monitoring software*   The other items in this list pertain to functionality – that of the Cloud environment. Each of these items is necessary for successful use of the Cloud environment. This last item pertains to monitoring the people who work for the CSP and interact with the Cloud environment. As the Roman poet Juvenal put it: *Quis custodiet ipsos custodes?* Loosely translated, this equates to: 'Who will guard the guardians?' End-users depend upon the Cloud provider to protect their applications from access or penetration by other entities. However, end-users also have questions about protecting their applications from inappropriate access by the Cloud service provider's employees. Consequently, many Cloud providers implement monitoring software that tracks interactions with key system components to ensure that only authorised personnel are accessing them. By reviewing the tracking software records, the Cloud provider can be sure that no unauthorised activity is taking place in its Cloud Computing environment.

In IaaS environments, the hypervisor represents the demarcation of the trust boundary. The Cloud provider is responsible for *the hypervisor and everything below it*, while the user is responsible for elements above the hypervisor.

Computing software infrastructure: Cloud user responsibility

Let's examine the Cloud Computing components the user is responsible for. It's critical to remember that one's application is running in someone else's computing environment, and, therefore, practices that were acceptable in an environment controlled by one are no longer applicable or appropriate. On the other hand, from the user's perspective, the management task is far simpler, since so many elements of the complete environment are another's responsibility – just look at the list of items described above to understand how much work is offloaded to the Cloud provider. So, in an IaaS environment provided by an external party, here are the portions of the overall system for which the user is responsible:

Operating system

The operating system forms the foundation for the user's application. From an application-execution perspective, there is no difference between an operating system running in one's own data centre on a physical server and an operating system running in a Cloud service provider's environment.

The operating system is a set of software services that enable user code to operate. Common operating system services include process launch, process scheduling and file system storage. A number of other system services that enable application code execution also are typically included in the operating system; for example, logging services that store entries reflecting system events. The aggregation of this software is referred to as the operating system.

In a Cloud Computing environment, security of the operating system is the responsibility of the user. This means that all responsibility for upgrades, patches, configuration and operations falls upon the user.

To a certain degree, this is common sense. The user decides on the operating system, installs the software and is responsible for running the application. Of course, the user is responsible for managing the application and responsible for the security of the operating system.

However, many application groups are accustomed to receiving pre-configured virtual machines from a central operations group, with subsequent management being the responsibility of operations.

In a Cloud environment, the applications group may implement an application with no interaction with an operations group and no subsequent involvement or support by that group. Or, the application implementer may mistakenly believe that the Cloud provider will take responsibility for operating system management. In this end, no one may end up ensuring that the operating system is upgraded, patched and managed appropriately.

Make no mistake, in a public IaaS environment, security of the operating system falls to the user.

Middleware

Middleware is a funny term, a portmanteau word that blends the latter part of the word 'software' with the location identifier 'middle'. For a putatively scientific field like software engineering, middleware seems like a very vague term.

The term was originally coined to represent software installed in an operating system that provides services to applications, but it not part of the application itself. For example, database software is often referred to as middleware, as are message queues, application servers or application development frameworks like Spring, and caching software.

As with the operating system, this software is under the control of the Cloud user, and responsibility for its security also lies with the user, not the Cloud provider.

Application code

Application code refers to the software components that provide the actual functionality of the application. This code may take the form of java components, web pages or standalone executable binaries. It is perhaps quite obvious that responsibility for the security of application code resides with the user of the Cloud service, not the provider.

Other application components

In a complex application topology, components of the application may reside in other virtual machines. Common examples of these components are load balancers, caching software like memcached, and billing software used to charge the ultimate end-users of the application for its use. These components provide application-level functionality, in contrast to middleware, which provides operating system-level functionality. These components may be installed as software packages by the Cloud user, or these components may be provided by the component creator in a preconfigured virtual machine template.

Whether the component is installed by the user or is launched by the user from a creator-created template, responsibility for its security resides with the user, unless the provider explicitly provides the service and offers support for it.

This implies that the end-user is ultimately responsible for the security of these components, despite the fact that the code may be created and released by another company (in fact, the same thing is true for middleware components sourced from a third party). This further implies that an organisation that uses third-party components in its application must have some mechanism to manage necessary security issues in these components. The mechanism may take the form of having possession of the component source code (as in the case of an open source product) or may take the form of a support contract from the component supplier.

No matter how the component is obtained, responsibility for its security lies with the user, and no provider will assume responsibility for security of these components. Please see the next section on templates for additional discussion about the use of externally sourced components.

Templates

Because the operating system is running in a virtualised environment, however, there can be significant differences regarding the provenance of the operating systems used by the application. Virtualisation supports the concept of a template – in effect, a base image that may be leveraged by a user to form the foundation of a new operating system to be executed in the virtualised environment. This is somewhat analogous to using a standardised form in a word processing program that then has document-specific information filled in for a particular use.

This template concept is extended in Cloud Computing. Most Cloud providers offer the ability to create a template, so that a standardised operating system build is used by, say, every application group in an organisation. This ensures consistency among all the organisation's applications, which is useful for operational simplicity. It also reduces work for people creating new applications; rather than having to create an application environment from scratch, developers can select an appropriate template, clone it and immediately begin productive work on their project. The ability to create templates to be shared within an organisation is often called 'private templates', as their use is limited to a single organisation.

Many Cloud providers also offer the ability for templates to be more widely shared in a format referred to as public templates. In this variant, templates are made available to be used by any user of the Cloud environment. The providers of these templates are commonly (but not exclusively) software vendors, who pre-populate the template with their installed and configured product. Using a software vendor's template offers the same kind of operational efficiency alluded to above; from the vendor's perspective, the practice induces trial, which may lead to increased sales.

The crucial issue relating to public templates is that such a template may be deliberately or inadvertently compromised with viruses, malware and the like. Moreover, if the template is poorly configured, security breaches may be possible.

Because of the possibility that a public template might be compromised, one might assume that organisations would avoid their use. Unfortunately, that assumption may not be appropriate. Someone may have begun using a public template as the basis for an application without realising the security exposure it presents. Or, someone may have begun using a public template with the intention of replacing its use later, but neglect to do so.

Certainly, an important concern for any organisation using an external provider is to ensure that any templates used are appropriate and secure – because, remember, in a public Cloud Computing environment, security above the hypervisor is the user's responsibility, not the provider's.

Licensing

One last item tangentially related to security, yet extremely important to applications, is software licensing. Software licences govern the use of software components, and complying with software licence conditions is an extremely important aspect of IT operations. The issue of software licensing in Cloud Computing environments can be quite complex. Nevertheless, it is clear that complying with the licensing conditions of software components is the responsibility of whoever is responsible for the provision of the resource that contains the component.

So, for example, the Cloud provider is responsible for complying with the licensing conditions of the hypervisor software, while the Cloud user is responsible for complying with the licensing conditions of user-installed middleware.

This rather neat bifurcation of licensing responsibility breaks down, however, when the Cloud provider delivers the software component. For example, many Cloud providers offer templates of virtual machines that have a Windows® operating system pre-installed; the user pays an hourly or monthly fee for use of the Windows® operating system within its application topology, while the Cloud provider pays Microsoft a licensing fee for the use of the operating system by the user. In a situation such as this, compliance with the software licence is the responsibility of the Cloud provider. In other words, while the user pays a fee for use of the Windows® operating systems, it is the responsibility of the Cloud provider to comply with all requirements and restrictions imposed by Microsoft relating to deployment of its operating system in the Cloud provider's environment.

Conclusion

This chapter has discussed how security in a Cloud Computing environment differs from that in a traditional dedicated data centre.

Part of the difference is due to the software technologies used to implement Cloud Computing environments. Virtualisation abstracts operating environments away from physical servers and makes assumptions about static computing environments obsolete. The automated orchestration aspects of Cloud environments means that manual implementation of security products, components, and configurations cannot keep up with dynamic topologies of Cloud applications.

Beyond the Cloud technology changes, Cloud Computing environments are also quite different from traditional data centres. Because Cloud environments are shared pools of resources, many traditional security practices based on placing appliances within the data centre are no longer tenable.

Finally, of course, Cloud Computing environments differ because part of the overall security responsibility lies with the Cloud provider, while another part lies with the Cloud users. This shared responsibility meets at the 'trust boundary', which demarcates which part is responsible for security in a particular 'layer' of the overall solution.

Figure 6 was introduced to illustrate the layers of the overall Cloud environment and to indicate where the trust boundary is located in a public IaaS environment.

Each layer of the environment was described, offering detail about security elements that make up the layer.

With this foundation of security knowledge, we can next turn to how IT organisations can evaluate security below the trust boundary. *Chapter 5* is devoted to understanding how evaluation may be performed and the crucial role of certification in Cloud security.

CHAPTER 5: ASSESSING SECURITY IN THE CLOUD

In *Chapter 4*, we discussed why Cloud Computing security is different from traditional approaches to computing security. Among the reasons cited were:

- *Virtualisation* Many traditional security solutions rely on examining network traffic. In virtualised environments, network traffic often goes from one virtual machine to another without leaving the physical server, rendering network-attached security devices ineffective.
- *Dynamic environments* Virtualisation environments support dynamic placement and relocation of virtual machines to enable hardware failure resiliency and better application performance. The side effect of this is that security practices that assume a static environment are challenged to operate effectively in a dynamic infrastructure.
- *Multi-tenant environments* Many security products and practices were designed for environments that are controlled by a single entity. In such environments, examining all network packets or performing port scanning is perfectly acceptable. In a multi-tenant Cloud environment, such approaches are often a violation of the provider's terms of service.

In Cloud Computing environments, the reality is that security is no longer the duty of a single entity. Instead, security is a shared responsibility: part of the responsibility lies with the Cloud provider, and part lies with the Cloud user. The question is, how does one assess the security of those portions of the Cloud Computing environment that lie within the responsibility area of the provider?

Assessing Cloud security

One approach, of course, would be to rely on the word of the provider. The provider would assert that everything in the environment is fine, security-wise, and the user would accept the assertion as definitive.

The problem with that approach is that, while the user would rely on the provider to implement security correctly, nearly all of the risk for any security issue falls upon the user of the service. If you look at 7*Figure 1*, first introduced in *Chapter 2*, you'll note that its implication is quite clear: while providers and users share responsibility for security and compliance, risk associated with failure lies primarily with the user.

In some sense, it may seem unfair that Cloud users bear risk responsibility for infrastructure elements out of their control, but that is the reality of how most Cloud service contracts are drawn up. However, just to reinforce a point made earlier, this asymmetric risk responsibility is not unique to Cloud Computing. Nearly every type of technology outsourcing contract is carefully drawn up by the provider to limit its risk exposure. In fact, one might infer that these contracts are deliberately drawn up to minimise the risk providers face and to shield themselves from any consequences that might arise from their actions.

Given this state of affairs, fair or not, users must recognise that the quality of the provider's security is important to them, and measures beyond blind faith are required. Failing to implement measures designed to minimise security, or compliance issues located within the provider's area of responsibility, raises the likelihood that the user will increase its overall risk.

Peeking below the trust boundary

Chapter 4 also further discussed the concept of a 'trust boundary' (*see Figure 6*). The trust boundary represents the interface that identifies where a user's responsibility for direct security implementation ends and where the provider's begins. If you look at the figure, you'll note that the actions identified below the trust boundary are 'evaluation and certification'.

What this means is that, in the absence of the ability to perform direct security actions (e.g. place a traffic sniffer on the internal data centre network), one must evaluate the measures the provider takes to secure the areas of its responsibility.

On its face, evaluation is a very clear concept: one observes the actions taken by another party and considers whether they are sufficient to implement the objectives of the observer. This practice is present in every situation in which one relies on another party to perform activities. For example, when one calls a plumber to come and fix a leaking pipe, before paying them, one evaluates whether the plumber has implemented fixing the pipe correctly.

The challenge of evaluation

Evaluation, however, can be a complex task. Even for something that, at first sight, seems like a straightforward situation to assess, evaluation can be very difficult. Take as an example, the plumbing evaluation just mentioned. While it might seem trivial to assess whether a plumber fits a pipe properly, even that task carries with it complexities like:

- Was the task performed correctly? It might not leak now, but did the plumber use techniques that will prevent leaks in the future? Did they use sealant that will stand up over time, or did they use cheap sealant that will break down quickly?
- Did they follow all applicable rules and regulations? Even for something as simple as a pipe (basically, a tube that allows a fluid to be sent from one place to another – what could be simpler?), there can be a number of regulations that are applicable – size, pipe composition, bracing (if necessary) and so on.
- Do they have all necessary licences and certifications? While many deride the over-regulation that occurs in many domains, licences and certifications are a fact of life. And the lack of a plumber's necessary licensing might become important in the event of an insurance claim or lawsuit.

Consequently, evaluation can be a very important and difficult proposition. And many organisations (and homeowners, in the case of plumbing!) find it difficult to conduct an appropriate evaluation. Some of the reasons are:

- *Lack of domain expertise* While it's easy to discern whether a pipe is leaking after the plumber concludes their work, a homeowner may not know all the applicable laws and regulations. For more complex matters like Cloud Computing, organisations may not have the knowledge base to discern whether a Cloud provider is doing a good job or not.

- *Applying expertise to a new domain* Even detailed knowledge about something fairly similar to a given domain may be insufficient for a new domain. Knowing a lot about water-oriented plumbing may not help in knowing enough about natural gas plumbing. In the case of Cloud Computing, knowing a lot about running a data centre may not be sufficient to understand compliance needs and best practices for operating a multi-tenant data centre environment.
- *Creating time to conduct a thorough evaluation* Everyone is busy, and IT organisations have been systematically squeezed of headcount. Most would find it difficult to divert staff to conduct a thorough Cloud security evaluation, just as most of us would find it difficult to find enough time, given our hectic lives, to fully assess the quality of a plumber's work.
- *Getting attention from the vendor* How can you get a rich enough interaction to ensure your evaluation obtains sufficient information to make the necessary assessment? It's an unfortunate fact of life that Cloud providers pay attention to their largest customers and minimise interaction with customers who represent small revenue opportunities – even if a thorough assessment is critical for that small opportunity customer. To be fair to Cloud providers, it's challenging for them to deal with an environment in which every customer or potential customer wants to conduct an evaluation. Every evaluation requires time and attention from provider personnel, and most of the evaluations will, ultimately, be nearly identical in 90% of the aspects they assess. Clearly, this repetitive evaluation process is inefficient. There should be a better way. Fortunately, there is.

Role of certification

Many industries confront the evaluation problems outlined above. How can buyers assess the quality of industry vendors, given the complexities and time constraints present in all businesses? How can vendors reduce the time devoted to evaluation in an environment in which many buyers want to perform similar evaluation processes?

The solution for most industries is to develop a set of recommended best practices promulgated by an impartial trade association, usually comprised of vendor and user representatives. The recommended best practices are typically characterised as a standard, indicating that all vendors that wish to be recognised as high quality must meet the requirements laid out in the standard.

Because IT systems often have financial implications due to their use in company operations, or as the system of record for financial transactions, the accounting industry often participates in these association efforts.

Alternatively, the accounting industry may itself develop and promulgate the recommended practices. In doing so, it would ordinarily create a body tasked with developing the standard; this body would include representatives from all interested parties, including the accounting industry, vendors, users and perhaps government agencies and regulatory bodies.

Once a standard is in place, it simplifies the evaluation process. Instead of each participant in an industry developing its own criteria, everyone can use the standard as the basis for evaluation.

Of course, having a common set of criteria doesn't solve the problem of each user conducting its own evaluation. If each potential customer seeks to conduct its own evaluation against the criteria, there is clearly an issue with redundancy of effort, which is inefficient and expensive. Moreover, the existence of a standard doesn't necessarily solve the problem of lack of user expertise – just because criteria have been established, doesn't mean that users have the knowledge base to understand the criteria or the judgement to assess a vendor's compliance with the standard.

Certifications and audits

Consequently, the standards process has taken the further step of establishing an audit process, designed to standardise the evaluation process.

A vendor can undergo an audit, whereby an external party will assess the vendor's compliance with the relevant standard, and pass judgement as to the level of compliance present in the vendor's environment.

The audit process simplifies things enormously. Instead of repetitive evaluations conducted by multiple customers, the vendor can undergo one evaluation process, at the end of which it receives a certificate of compliance with the standard. Any subsequent customer who wishes to establish the vendor's compliance with the standard can accept the certification as proof that the vendor meets the standard's requirements.

Of course, this raises the question: who is able to conduct such an audit and how can that organisation be trusted to do a good job?

The answer, naturally enough, is that the body that promulgated the standard certifies the auditing organisation.

The auditor goes through a process designed to ensure that it has the expertise and thoroughness to fully evaluate a vendor's compliance with the standard. As the end of the process, the auditor is certified as being capable of performing audits against the standard and, crucially, able to provide the vendor being evaluated with a certificate of standard compliance.

How certifications work

Certification refers to a process whereby a provider has an external auditor examine a given domain and evaluate it against a formal set of criteria. These criteria are typically created by an independent industry body, thereby assuring objectivity and impartiality in the criteria definition.

The external auditor gains access to the provider's infrastructure and assesses its practices according to the criteria defined in the particular certification domain. After the audit is complete, if the provider's practices meet the requirements of the audit, the auditor issues a report detailing the provider's compliance with the certification criteria. The shorthand phrase for this process is that the provider is certified against a particular audit process.

Once a provider has undergone the audit process and received a certification, it can present itself as certified for a particular domain. In turn, customers or potential customers of that provider can accept the certification in place of performing their own audit.

As can be seen, the certification process neatly addresses the issues regarding user evaluation identified earlier in this chapter. Rather than attempting to create and perform its own audit, a customer or potential customer can identify the key audit/certification domains relevant to its needs and request those from service providers.

Many companies considering using an external provider go even further: they insist that providers, in order to be considered as a potential choice, must have undergone specific audit processes and offer proof of successfully achieving certification.

As one can easily imagine, the ability to rely on impartial audit requirements and associated certificates can simplify the evaluation process enormously.

Common certification processes germane to Cloud Computing include:

- *COBIT (IT Governance and Control)* This set of requirements relates to how IT organisations are managed, including how internal processes are defined and enforced.
- *HIPAA (Health Insurance Portability and Accountability Act)* This Act sets out a number of requirements relating to information privacy. As suggested by its name, HIPAA is focused specifically on health care and affects organisations of many different types involved in the medical field.
- *SP 800-53* This NIST (National Institute of Standards and Testing) Special Publication focuses on security controls for IT environments. NIST published this as a guide to help government organisations prepare to undergo audits performed under the Federal Information Security Management Act (FISMA). While the titles of the organisation and the Act suggest this affects only government bodies, service providers that seek to host federal government applications need to meet FISMA

requirements, so this standard is germane to CSPs, as well as government agencies.

- *FedRAMP* The Federal Risk and Authorization Management Program is an initiative sponsored by the federal government to make the audit process easier for government agencies and CSPs. The FISMA standard outlined above requires every application to undergo a security audit, part of which assesses the infrastructure upon which the application resides. Obviously, if a large number of applications need to be audited in a process that is largely repetitive with respect to the infrastructure, this is inefficient and costly. FedRAMP is an effort to streamline this process and enable a single audit process to be used by multiple FISMA efforts.

- *PCI-DSS* The Payment Card Industry Data Security Standard is a standard associated with taking electronic payments. Obviously, there are important requirements in the area of security and privacy with respect to financial transactions, and PCI sets out the requirements in this domain.

- *ISO27001* (full title: ISO/IEC 27001:2005 Information technology – Security techniques – Information security management systems – Requirements) This standard, published by the International Standards Organisation, sets out security controls designed to ensure that IT organisations have a defined and consistent approach to information security.

- *BITS* BITS is part of the Financial Institution Shared Assessments Program and is designed to help assess the security controls of IT service providers. From the name of the sponsoring organisation, it is obvious that this is oriented toward the financial services industry. This initiative is analogous to the FISMA and FedRAMP audit standards described above.

- *SAS 70* (full title: Statement on Auditing Standards (SAS) No. 70, Service Organisations)   Note that SAS 70 was superseded by SSAE 16 (full title: Reporting on Controls at a Service Organisation) in mid-2011 and will be the appropriate certification going forward. SAS 70 and its successor provide an assessment of the processes a provider follows in delivering a service. This assessment ensures that processes are defined explicitly and that the provider has measures in place to ensure that they are consistently executed.
- *GAPP*   The Generally Accepted Privacy Principles are a set of measures formulated by the American Institute of CPAs (AICPA) directed toward IT privacy practices and policies. As can be seen from its title, GAPP is directed toward some of the same objectives as HIPAA.

Dealing with multiple compliance standards

There is an old joke in the IT industry that standards are great and that's why there's so many of them. The joke illustrates what must be obvious from the list in the last section: there are lots of compliance requirements, some generally applicable and others focused on specific industries. Intuitively, there must be significant overlap among the different compliance regimes.

Consequently, while in the abstract the existence of audit requirements and certifications seems that it would make life simple for IT users, it would be more appropriate to say that it makes life simpler.

While audits and certifications may address the detailed specifics of security and privacy, which is certainly a huge benefit, they still present an IT organisation with the need to assess which compliance standards are appropriate for its specific environment.

Moreover, if multiple compliance requirements are germane for the IT organisation, the obvious question is how to ensure that every element of each requirement is addressed without having to repetitively run through each audit standard.

Finally, even if an IT organisation is able to understand how to manage each of the audit standards appropriate to its specific situation, it is still faced with the need to understand how to apply them to a CSP's Cloud offering.

Cloud Security Alliance

Fortunately, companies seeking to sort out Cloud Computing security and compliance don't have to fight the battle alone. The Cloud Security Alliance (typically referred to as CSA) is an organisation that provides a locus of research, expertise and recommendations in the area of Cloud security. The CSA is located at *https://cloudsecurityalliance.org/*.

Founded in 2008, the CSA is a not-for-profit organisation with a mission 'to promote the use of best practices for providing security assurance within Cloud Computing, and provide education on the uses of Cloud Computing to help secure all other forms of computing'.

The CSA is the centre of gravity with respect to the topic of Cloud Computing security. It is comprised of end-users, vendors and service providers, all of whom interact in the interest of defining what Cloud Computing security requires and how to achieve it.

CSA has an international scope, and has both national and local chapters. Anyone seeking to understand the nuances of Cloud security and to learn current best practices should consider getting involved in the CSA. It sponsors a yearly Cloud security conference in November; if you are someone seeking deeper involvement in Cloud Computing security, this conference is a must-attend event.

Leveraging the CSA

In addition to its overall security focus, the CSA has published research documents focused on easing the audit and compliance complexity faced by Cloud users.

As a general overview of how security and compliance relate to Cloud Computing, the CSA published the 'Guidance for Critical Areas of Focus in Cloud Computing'. This document discusses how Cloud Computing relates to 13 different security and compliance areas, including governance and risk management, interoperability and portability, and data centre operations, to name but three.

The 'Guidance' document provides an excellent overview and jumping-off point to better understand the landscape of Cloud Computing security.

With respect to specific aspects of assessing the security of a CSP, two further CSA documents are highly valuable for IT organisations. The documents also provide guidance on how to map the most relevant audit standards to one another.

The first document is the Consensus Assessments Initiative Questionnaire (CAI), published in late 2010. This questionnaire 'provides a set of questions a Cloud consumer and Cloud auditor may wish to ask of a Cloud provider. It provides a series of yes or no control assertion questions which can then be tailored to suit each unique Cloud customer's evidentiary requirements.'

The second document is The CSA Cloud Controls Matrix (CCM), which provides a 'controls framework that gives detailed understanding of security concepts and principles that are aligned to the Cloud Security Alliance guidance in 13 domains'. The CCM was first published in April 2010, and has subsequently been updated, with the latest version released in August 2011.

All three of these documents may be found at *https://cloudsecurityalliance.org/research/*.

Overview of the CAI and CCM

The purpose of both the CAI and CCM is to provide guidance and recommendations in a number of specific areas for IT organisations wishing to audit CSPs and assess their security practices.

The two documents share a common taxonomy of security aspects, which makes it easy to cross-correlate the security requirements (the controls) to assess how well the CSP implements them (the questionnaire).

The security aspects of the two documents are as follows:

- compliance
- data governance
- facility security

- human resources
- information security
- legal
- operations management
- risk management
- release management
- resiliency
- security architecture.

Each of these areas has one or more individual items associated with it. For example, release management has five separate items:

- new development/acquisition
- production changes
- quality testing
- outsourced development
- unauthorised software installations.

The CCM outlines the control requirements for each item in a matrix. These requirements are assertions about how a CSP should comply with the individual item.

The CAI contains the same areas and items, but lists a set of questions to be posed to a CSP for each item to assist in determining whether the CSP meets the requirements outlined in the CCM. This list of questions helps IT organisations formulate an organisation-specific audit – they provide the foundation for a complete set of questions that will reflect the organisation's audit and compliance requirements.

A number of compliance standards relevant to Cloud Computing were outlined earlier in this chapter. As noted, some of them overlap. Furthermore, for an individual IT organisation, figuring out which parts of each standard are relevant and how they relate to the CSA's security areas and items would seem challenging, to say the least.

Fortunately, the CSA has made this challenge much simpler. Both the CAI and CCM contain columns for each security standard. For every security item outlined in the documents, the relevant portions of each standard are called out. For example, for the item ownership/stewardship within the data governance area, the COBIT column notes as relevant areas COBIT 4.1 DS5.1 and PO 2.3.

The benefit this set of columns provides for IT organisations is immense. Rather than having to work through each relevant compliance standard and assess which part of each standard is appropriate to different audit areas, the organisation can rely on the list the CSA has put together. This simplifies the audit task enormously. Of course, it is still necessary to interact with individual CSPs and work through the audit process, but an evaluation framework makes the audit process easier.

The CSA and its CAI and CCM provide an excellent set of resources for the very important security issues associated with using a CSP. The CAI and CCM are, as just noted, a foundation for the audit process itself. Naturally, individual organisations may find it necessary to identify additional audit items or may be subject to additional compliance standard requirements, but the two documents offer an excellent starting point.

Mapping the CAI and CCM to the security stack

For many people, particularly those for whom security is not a primary focus or strength, the organisation of the CAI and CCM may be problematic. While the taxonomy areas of the documents may make sense to security professionals, IT personnel in the applications and infrastructure/operations areas may be more comfortable evaluating security in terms of a security stack, much like the one presented in *Figure 6* of *Chapter 4*.

This poses a problem since the items within the CAI and CCM are organised topically (i.e. information governance) and not according to where each item falls within the architecture stack. For IT organisations that assign security responsibility according to which part of the stack the security item resides, a mapping of the CSA areas and items to the stack is useful.

Table 1 lists each part of the security stack and identifies which item(s) from the CAI and CCM are associated with it. This structure will aid IT organisations as they work through audit processes and assign individuals to participate in the process.

Table 1

Security layer	Consensus assessment initiative section(s)
General security policy	Compliance 01–08
	Legal 01–02
	Human resources 01–03
	Information security 01–16, 22–27, 32
	Operations management 01

	Release management 01
	Resiliency 01–02
	Risk management 01–05
	Security 01
Facility and facility computing infrastructure	Facility security 01–08
	Resiliency 03–08
Facility Computing Infrastructure	Data governance 01–08
	Information security 04, 09–10, 18–19, 23, 28–32
	Operations management 02–03, 05
	Risk management 05
	Release management 01
	Security 03, 05, 10–13,
Facility Software Infrastructure	Information security 04, 07–10, 17 20–21, 29, 32–34
	Release management 02–05
	Security 02, 04, 06–09, 14–15
	Operations management 04

Conclusion

This chapter has focused on evaluating CSP security. It began by identifying why virtualisation and Cloud Computing present challenges to established IT security practices.

As noted, virtualisation itself poses challenges to traditional security practices. Abstracting dependence upon physical devices offers significant operational and financial benefits, but can prevent common practices like packet inspection from operating properly.

The concept of the trust boundary was introduced, with the corresponding fact that using a CSP prevents direct application of many common security solutions. For example, lacking control of the computing environment, security groups cannot take advantage of solutions like placing intrusion detection and prevention appliances on the network.

The existence of the trust boundary means that IT organisations must rely on evaluation and certifications when it comes to assessing the security of a CSP. Understanding, not to say implementing, a CSP audit process is in itself a challenge, with problems posed by the need to develop Cloud-specific knowledge, as well as understanding and interpreting individual compliance standards.

Fortunately, organisations recognising the challenges caused by Cloud Computing security came together to form the Cloud Security Alliance. Beyond offering a gathering point for users, vendors and service providers to collaborate in this area, the CSA has published research documents offering guidance on evaluating CSP security.

Two relevant CSA documents were discussed: the Consensus Assessments Initiative and the Cloud Controls Matrix. Use of these documents can simplify and accelerate evaluation of a CSP's security practices and also build confidence on the part of users that the CSP has implemented appropriate practices.

Finally, for those for whom a security evaluation organised according to a stack architecture is more comfortable, a mapping from the security stack first presented in *Chapter 4* to the CSA evaluation documents was presented in table format.

Using these tools, one's confidence in a CSP's security practices can be increased. For many, this would seem to complete the topic of Cloud security – for them, all security issues rest with the provider and are the provider's responsibility.

Of course, that is too simple and convenient a position. Most providers, while implementing (and demonstrating, via the evaluation process described in this chapter) appropriate security practices, unmistakeably reduce their risk exposure, leaving the majority of risk for any security issues with the user.

Beyond the obvious business motivation for this – it makes perfect sense to reduce one's exposure to risk – there is another very good reason why CSPs insist on risk limitation. The reason is that the CSP's Cloud environment does not exist in isolation – there is always an application that is part of the equation. And no CSP can (nor should it) take on responsibility for the security of a user's application. No user wants to allow a third party (i.e. the CSP) to rifle through its code or data; consequently, the CSP quite rightly disavows any responsibility for the security of the application. Application security is explicitly left to the user, which causes its own set of problems.

Just as infrastructure security practices must change in a CSP setting, so too must application security practices. Many IT organisations fail to understand this, to their peril. Identifying and implementing appropriate application security practices is critical in a Cloud Computing environment, and it is to that subject we turn in the next chapter.

CHAPTER 6: CLOUD COMPUTING APPLICATION SECURITY

We concluded *Chapter 5* by noting that CSPs view security (quite rightly) as a shared responsibility. A CSP may be quite willing to accept responsibility for the security measures that lie on its side of the trust boundary, but it will (also quite rightly) abjure any responsibility for the security of an application deployed by a third party.

That attitude certainly makes sense; after all, the CSP has no insight into the development practices, testing regimen or operational processes of the application's owner – how can it possibly accept responsibility for its security?

This bifurcation of security responsibilities is illustrated in *Figure 7*, which was also presented in *Chapter 4*. The figure portrays the stack of functionality that makes up a Cloud Computing application. At the bottom is the facility in which the infrastructure and hardware reside that make up the physical assets of the computing environment. At the top is the application software that provides business functionality for the application's owner.

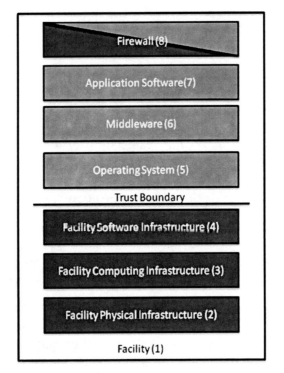

Figure 7: Stack of elements to deliver application functionality

Between Layers 4 and 5 of the stack is the trust boundary that divides security responsibility between the Cloud provider and Cloud users.

One key fact all Cloud users confront is that, unlike environments in which they own and manage the data centre in which an application operates, in a public Cloud environment users have no control over the security of portions of the stack below the trust boundary. Instead of implementing their own security practices, users must, instead, rely on the security measures implemented by the Cloud provider.

For those elements of the stack that lie below the trust boundary, users must find other methods to establish confidence in the security practices applied to that portion of the infrastructure. While blind confidence in the Cloud provider's security is possible, most Cloud users rely on a combination of evaluation and certification. *Chapter 5* discussed the process of evaluation and certification extensively, and presented mechanisms to accomplish evaluation and certification. The Cloud Security Alliance Consensus Assessments Initiative and the complementary Cloud Controls Matrix were pointed to as excellent resources to assist in this effort.

For many IT organisations, this is where security validation ends. Once the provider's security practices are validated, these organisations assume that everything is OK and endorse deployment of applications into the Cloud provider's environment.

This, however, is an inappropriate response and one that reflects a shortfall in good security practices. As a figure presented in *Chapter 2* and reproduced here as *Figure 8* illustrates, Cloud security is a shared responsibility. Furthermore, just as the unique characteristics of Cloud Computing affect the security practices of the Cloud provider, so too do they affect the security practices of the Cloud user.

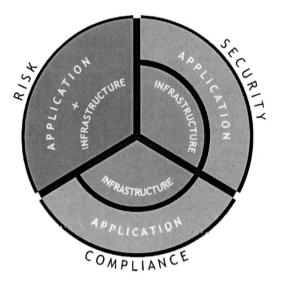

Figure 8: Risk, security and compliance

Why is this?

It's important to understand the effect of operating an application in a third-party shared environment:

- *Restricted deployment* Many security products cannot be deployed in a shared environment. This means that security practices that assume, for example, that a security appliance can be installed in the data centre and used as a shared security resource by all applications is not longer tenable.

- *Dangerous neighbours* Applications deployed in a corporate data centre assume that other applications also residing in the data centre are friendly – that is, they are non-malevolent and unlikely to be a security danger. In a Cloud environment, one cannot assume friendly neighbours; moreover, even if the neighbours are non-malevolent, they may implement poor security practices that, if not protected against by appropriate practices in one's own application, might leave the application vulnerable.

- *Porous security perimeter* Traditionally, many IT organisation security practices concentrated on the edge of the data centre. Secure that from penetration, went the thinking, and internal resources can be assumed to be safe from malicious intent. Whether that sort of thinking was ever appropriate is subject to debate, but that thinking is clearly out of date. Most IT organisations now deliberate allow external access into their data centres to customers and partners. The phenomenon is so widespread, in fact, that the well-known security consortium refers to it as 'the deperimeterisation of security'.

For all of these reasons, Cloud application security must be managed differently. Organisations must develop an appropriate application security that takes the unique characteristics of Cloud Computing into account and implements appropriate security practices on their side of the trust boundary.

There are six areas that IT organisations must address to ensure appropriate application security in Cloud environments. These six areas are:

Identity management and role-based access controls This security element addresses user application access; in other words, who has access to the application to use it, and how is that access managed and made secure?

Another aspect of this element is managing who has administrative access to the application and the virtual machine (or instance) that it runs on. An important issue in this regard is changing administrative access rights throughout the life cycle of the application; it may be appropriate for a developer to have access to core system services during development or testing, but completely inappropriate for them to have system access when the application is in production.

Network security   In a Cloud environment, network traffic flows to and from the application across the Internet. After traffic access the application from outside the Cloud data centre, traffic flows across the Cloud's internal data network, which is shared with traffic from other user's applications.

As noted earlier in this chapter, one cannot assume that other user's applications are safe, so it is critical that one's application's traffic is safe from malevolent access.

Data security   As discussed in the last chapter, Cloud providers have responsibility for the security of the hardware computing infrastructure. That, of course, includes the storage infrastructure.

Nevertheless, storage is a shared resource in which one organisation's data is stored adjacent to another's data. And whatever security measures the Cloud provider has implemented might not be implemented properly, leaving an organisation's data vulnerable to being accessed by someone else.

Furthermore, even if the Cloud provider's security practices prevent access by an inappropriate user, this still leaves the issue that data is accessible to the Cloud provider itself. This type of access is made worse by the fact that the Cloud provider may be forced to offer access to the data to a governmental body due to a subpoena – in other words, the Cloud provider may be legally forced to provide access to one's data.

In some situations, the fact that access to the data may not even be disclosed to the user is definitely disquieting. For all these reasons, preventing access to one's data is crucial.

Instance security Restricted deployment options, noisy neighbours and the deperimeterisation make it clear that virtual machine security must be implemented at the application level. This typically means that each instance (virtual machine) in an application must implement sufficient security measures to protect itself against attack, malware and the like.

Application architecture and deployment topology Even if every application instance implements security measures sufficient to protect itself against attacks, a risk still exists that should one instance be successfully attacked, the attacker could use that beachhead to gain access to other instances or critical data. Therefore, it is important to implement application architectures that reduce the risk of attackers 'hopping' from a compromised instance to other instances.

Code update and patch management As a final element of application security, code and patch management is very important. Running insecure code in an environment that, by definition is populated by other users about whom little is known, presents a significant risk. Ensuring that both system assets (e.g. operating system services) and other code artefacts (i.e. middleware and application code) are patched as necessary is critical to operate in this shared environment.

Unfortunately, many organisations deploying applications into shared Cloud environments may fail to implement proper processes to ensure that code updates and patches are applied in a timely fashion.

The reasons for this vary. One reason is that it is often application groups that deploy these applications, and they commonly rely on an operations group to deploy code updates and patches. In an environment in which the operations group may not be involved in the project at all, this means that the patch processes may not ever be implemented.

Another reason Cloud applications often fail to be updated properly is that application groups may 'burn' an image (i.e. create a virtual machine template) that contains all the code assets that an instance requires to perform its function. Given the complexity of gathering all the assets and deploying the resulting image, Cloud applications may be updated infrequently, leaving them with security vulnerabilities.

A third reason that Cloud applications often fail to be updated properly is due to human error. In complex Cloud application topologies, there may be numerous instances in a product environment, with those instances taking on different roles and, therefore, carrying different code artefacts. In such a complex environment, the potential for human error during a code update process is manifest, thereby leaving the application with a security vulnerability.

These six areas represent the areas that application groups must address in order to ensure that their applications are secure when operating in a Cloud Computing environment. Failing to address one of more of the areas presents a risk that something untoward may occur. Just to reiterate the information discussed earlier in the chapter: when operating in a Cloud environment, a trust boundary exists. On one side of the trust boundary, security is the responsibility of the Cloud provider, and a user's responsibility is quite limited. The Cloud provider must take whatever security measures it deems appropriate; the user's actions are to evaluate and assess whether those measures are sufficient for the user's objectives.

On the other side of the trust boundary, security is the responsibility of the Cloud user. The provider cannot possibly take responsibility for security of code assets that the user controls and deploys.

Consequently, in order to ensure that the highest possible level of security for an application is implemented and that risk is reduced as much as practicable, Cloud users need to ensure that they implement appropriate security measures. These measures need to respect the limitations imposed by the Cloud environment, as well as ensure they align with the realities of how applications operate in that environment.

Let's look at the individual security elements that Cloud users must address for their applications.

Identity management and role-based access controls

Even though this is one element, it addresses two different groups: application users and application administrators. The security needs and practices for them differ because their interaction with the application is quite different.

User identity management

The security issue around user identity management is obvious: access to the application must be controlled with measures to ensure that only appropriate people access it as users, and whoever accesses the system as a user is able to use it only as appropriate to their role.

The challenge with user identity management results from the fact that Cloud applications run externally to the corporate data centre, where the company's identity management system typically resides. Consequently, the identity management mechanisms in the Cloud application do not have direct access to the corporate identity management environment (that is to say, the Cloud application resides outside the perimeter of the corporate data centre).

One way to address this problem is to have each Cloud application contain its own user identity management. Each user would have a login/password on each application and would use the login/password to access the application. Of course, that poses two problems:

- Users have login and password combinations on every application, which means each time a user accesses an application they have to type a login and password. Clearly, this is inconvenient to users.
- More worryingly, distributed identity management systems pose an obvious security risk. If a user leaves an organisation, their access rights to applications need to be revoked; if the organisation's identity management systems are located on every application, each application must be accessed and the user's login removed. Should one or more applications be

overlooked, the ex-employee would still be able to access the application.

The solution is evident: use a single identity management system to control application access by users.

Depending upon the organisation, the internal identity management system may or may not be accessible from outside the corporate data centre. Commonly, however, the corporation will not allow external access via the native ports used by the identity management system because it prefers to limit all external access through the data centre firewall other than that via the standard web ports (80 for HTTP; 443 for HTTPS).

One alternative is to place the identity management system or a copy of it outside the core of the data centre but still within the overall control of the company in an area commonly referred to as the DMZ (demilitarised zone). The purpose of the DMZ is to allow access to systems that need access from outside the company, but to ensure that no external access goes directly into the core data centre. All access to core systems goes through a system located in the DMZ, which in turn accesses – on behalf of the outside requester – internal systems. This scheme is a tried and trusted approach often used for company websites.

This DMZ approach addresses the issue of multiple identity management systems. However, many companies are reluctant to expose a copy of a critical company asset like the identity management system to external access. If companies are reluctant to place a copy of a core system into a location that is publicly accessible, obviously placing the core system itself there would be intolerable.

Even if a company is amenable to placing some sort of identity management system in a publicly accessible location, one problem still remains. Each time someone accesses a system that needs to authenticate and authorise the person, they need to re-enter credentials to gain access. If they need to access a number of systems, this repetitive effort becomes annoying. Even worse, it encourages password re-use among systems, which poses security issues.

One solution to the multiple sign-on issue, as it's referred to, is to, not surprisingly, implement a single sign-on system (SSO). As one can imagine, this is a fairly complex problem, calling for encryption, assurance that the central identity management system accessed is the right one, integration with the Cloud-based system and so on. Since the whole goal of an SSO system is to support many systems, so that the value of the single sign-on is maximised, having multiple incompatible SSO systems would be extremely undesirable.

Fortunately, a standard called SAML (Security Assertion Markup Language) has been established to support consistency in SSO implementation. Based on XML, SAML defines a protocol and process to support SSO. Even better, it is designed to leverage HTTP, making it possible to run its traffic across port 80, which most companies allow access into their DMZ.

SAML depends upon one site being able to verify from an established site the authentication of an individual. Therefore, it requires that a particular identity management system operates as the locus of authentication and authorisation. Assuming that the individual seeking access to another system is authenticated by the original identity management system, SAML operates to confirm the individual's identity and enable appropriate access to the second system.

SAML is the most widely accepted solution to the challenges of identity management in Cloud Computing, although it is by no means universally implemented. Many companies still suffer with multiple, distributed identity management systems, with all the associated issues outlined earlier. SAML provides real benefits, but achieving them requires investment in both software and staff time. One can expect that SAML will become more widely used in the future, and will represent the best practice in identity management.

Administrator identity management

The security issue regarding administrator identity management is different from that of users. While user identity management revolves around controlling access to an application, for administrators, identity management is concerned with controlling access to the instance and its system resources. For example, it is important that only appropriate administrative personnel can access an instance and perform management functions on a running database.

Administrative access requirements get even more complex when one addresses the fact that, depending upon where an application is in its life cycle, administrative access rules might be different.

As an example, consider a company's website. While it is in development, it is appropriate for software engineers to have administrative access to the instances that comprise the website. After all, the engineers need to install and configure application software components, not to mention configuring operating system software components like the instance's web server.

When that website moves into staging – that is, when it is deployed in a production-like environment for final testing – it may be appropriate for software engineers to have administrative access to the system. It may also be appropriate for operations personnel to have access to the system, so that they may learn about the configuration necessary for the application to run, as well as prepare the application to go into production.

When the application goes into production, however, it may no longer be appropriate for software engineers to have administrative access to the system. Many companies have explicit rules proscribing administrative access to production systems except for operations personnel.

Summed up, identity management for administrative personnel requires the ability to modify administrative access for application instances to manage it across its life cycle. Moreover, best practices also dictate that each person, no matter which role they represent, use a unique ID, so that system access may be tracked and audited.

The challenge for companies is that many Cloud providers use SSH to manage administrative access to Linux servers (for Windows® servers it is typical to use a Remote Desktop served up via the RDP protocol to control administrative access to servers; of course, this just displaces the need to manage administrative access to instances across the application life cycle and causes it to need to be managed in the Windows® user management system).

SSH is a very secure access mechanism in which all interaction between the remote client machine and a server is encrypted, with initial access based on whether the client machine can provide a private key that the instance recognises as matched to a public key located on the instance.

Unfortunately, this approach poses a problem: only one key matches the public key. This means that all personnel administering the machine must share a single key, which conflicts with the best practice of every administrator having a unique access mechanism to allow tracking and auditing.

One way to address this is to configure the instance to support multiple keys and ensure that each person accessing the system use a unique key. If appropriate logging is set up, then actions by each individual can be tracked, with the log used for any subsequent auditing that is necessary.

It should be obvious what the shortcoming in this approach is: the need to track which keys should be inserted into an instance, so that appropriate personnel have access and inappropriate personnel have no access. Any time manual processes are used to manage a security process such as this, it is likely to result in mistakes or deliberate evasion.

Consequently, many organisations turn to management frameworks to manage keys (and other things as well – we will return to the topic of management frameworks again in this chapter). The management framework is used to define a configuration for each instance in the application topology. Part of the configuration enables key management, with specific keys inserted according to the configuration. Moreover, the configuration can be defined flexibly enough, so that the individual keys inserted can be different according to where in its life cycle the application is. This flexibility can be used to allow developers access to instances early in the application life cycle, while preventing their access late in the life cycle, when only operations personnel are allowed access.

These management frameworks are extremely helpful in enforcing best practices and organisational policies. Rather than depending upon individuals to perform manual configuration every time an instance is launched, with the concomitant likelihood of errors, the framework is configured during application design and thereafter automatically executes the configuration each time an instance is launched. Furthermore, if the organisation decides to change its policy or needs to address the fact that someone with administrative access left the organisation, making a change to the configuration can be done easily and in one place. Finally, management frameworks support the requirement for access rights assigned according to the role of the user. Some users will be allowed to access only application artefacts, while others will be allowed access to system resources as well.

Identity management conclusion

As can be seen from this discussion, Cloud Computing presents significant challenges to the established mechanisms most companies use to control access to application and system software components.

Avoiding 'identity management system sprawl,' while also avoiding the need for users to continually login each time they access a new system, requires a rethink of how to manage identity and authentication. A number of technical approaches are possible, but most of them require changes to existing procedures. A method of managing this is represented by 'single sign-on,' using identity management systems that support the SAML standard.

Network security

The second of the six core Cloud application security issues is network security.

Just as with identity and authentication management, Cloud Computing presents challenges to network security assumptions and practices. There are straightforward mechanisms to address these challenges, but they require that additional tasks and processes be added to existing practices.

The challenge that Cloud Computing presents in network security is obvious: within a Cloud service provider environment, all application traffic runs along a shared network. One application's packets are intermingled with other application packets, all within a single network.

Of course, most Cloud providers will implement virtual LAN (VLAN) functionality, which segregates traffic by Cloud user. VLANs ensure that traffic intended for one user's virtual machines is not direct to another user's as well. To be frank, however, while VLAN technology is useful, it is a technique to virtually segregate traffic; the reality is that traffic still flows along a shared network, and if one feels that co-mingling packets is unacceptable, VLANs are unlikely to be sufficient to assuage that concern.

This situation is unlike that of a dedicated corporate data centre, in which all traffic is associated with a single entity.

In most corporate data centres, no effort is made to segregate traffic from different users. So, for example, packets from human resource applications are mixed with packets from finance applications. Moreover, typically users are unconcerned that system administrators might have access to the application packets, assuming a level of trust in administrator honesty.

A Cloud service provider environment, therefore, is perceived as significantly different from a corporate data centre environment. Many Cloud users feel that the security of VLAN techniques and the trustworthiness of administrators cannot be assumed; therefore, they seek methods to ensure that network traffic is protected from access by other users and Cloud service provider personnel.

Given that Cloud users have no access to or control over the Cloud provider's network, implementing separate physical network configurations is out of the question. Since the software techniques used by Cloud service providers like VLAN still present risk of network traffic access (at least for some users), users must turn to something that addresses the traffic itself, i.e. the packets that contain user data and travel across the Cloud provider's network.

The best technique to ensure that one's packets are safe from inappropriate access is to encrypt all traffic between application instances. This approach is often referred to as 'security for data in motion', referencing the fact that it addresses application data that is being transmitted along the network. There are a variety of commercial and open source software products that provide network data encryption, and one of them should be implemented to ensure network traffic is protected.

For some organisations, concern with security for data in motion applies more widely than just within the Cloud provider's data centre. For these organisations, the fact that access to the application flows across the public Internet is a concern. There are two methods to protect the security of packets travelling to and from the Cloud provider:

- Implement a private network connection to the Cloud provider. Rather than relying on the public Internet connection that mixes packets from many different organisations, a Cloud user can lease a private line from a network provider and send all traffic to and from the Cloud provider across the private line.

- Implement a virtual private network (VPN) connection to the Cloud provider. A VPN creates a connection between two endpoints (in this situation, the user's premises and the Cloud provider's data centre), using encryption to negate any possibility that an external entity can 'listen in' to the user's traffic flowing across the Internet. VPN technology is very well-established. All that needs to be done is to confirm the Cloud provider can terminate a VPN at their data centre perimeter; alternatively, one can terminate the VPN at an instance running within one's application topology. The latter would, for best practices, isolate the VPN technology in a server separate from the other application instances. Implementing a VPN from company premises to the Cloud provider's data centre and encrypting traffic within the provider's data centre offers the greatest security for data in motion. This approach reduces risk from inappropriate access to network traffic to a minimum.

Network security conclusion

The traditional argument against encryption is that it imposes a performance penalty due to the processing overhead of encryption and decryption. It is impossible to predict exactly what effect encryption will have on a specific application; the only sure way to characterise encryption overhead is to implement it and then execute performance testing, comparing the results to performance experienced with a non-encrypted environment.

Rather than assuming the need for encryption, a better approach is to evaluate the risk profile of the information flowing across the network. For some applications, security of data is paramount; for others, it is less so. With a risk profile in hand with which to assess the need for network security, and performance testing results also available, one can evaluate whether to implement network traffic encryption. It may be that only portions of an application's topology require traffic encryption, or perhaps portions of the company's application portfolio. A risk assessment that evaluates cost and complexity against the need for network security will offer guidance about the appropriate actions to take.

Data security

Data is, perhaps, the key asset in information technology. So much so that companies that suffer a catastrophic data centre loss that results in on-site data being lost due to storage equipment destruction often go out of business, crippled by their inability to reconstruct their data.

As a key asset, data must be managed carefully. Clearly, having an offsite back-up process is a fundamental requirement. Beyond that, however, it's critical that data be protected appropriately, just like any other important corporate asset. Data must be protected from theft and tampering, with inappropriate access prevented to ensure that the asset is protected.

Furthermore, for many companies, as discussed in the previous chapter, there are legal and regulatory requirements addressing data. Not only do these companies need to take appropriate measures to protect their data, they are subject to additional restrictions on how data must be accessed, protected and even disposed of. So, for many companies, there is an overlay of data security requirements on top of the common practices.

Placing this subject in the context of a Cloud provider further complicates the topic of data security. The fact that a company's data is located in a site under the control of another entity makes managing data security more complex. If you'll remember from the previous chapter, storage hardware is located beneath the trust boundary and is, therefore, the responsibility of the Cloud provider.

This means that company's seeking to use Cloud Computing must evaluate how to implement appropriate storage data security. This is commonly referred to as 'data at rest', indicating that the data is not being operated on (i.e. processed within a virtual machine instance) or being transmitted (i.e. sent along the network).

The issue of data security is made more challenging by the fact that storing it in an external Cloud provider means non-company personnel can access it. The typical assumption by most companies is that access by company personnel is low-risk, with little likelihood of inappropriate use of company data. In fact, that assumption is incorrect, as many data breaches occur when company personnel make inappropriate use of their employer's data.

Notwithstanding this, when external parties have access to a company's data because it is stored in a Cloud provider's environment, additional issues are present. While the provider's personnel may be trustworthy, with the provider implementing thorough screening of the personnel, most Cloud users feel that this situation presents additional risk when compared with storing data in the company's own data centre.

With regard to addressing legal and regulatory compliance issues relating to data storage, the reader is directed to the previous chapter. The CSA guidance discussed there has recommendations and controls addressing how a provider's data storage practices can be audited and assessed. As noted in the chapter, it may be that a specific company's situation may bring additional regulatory or legal requirements into play, and companies should be prepared to assess their own requirements beyond those addressed by the CSA to ensure that the provider's measures satisfy the user's requirements.

However, even if a provider implements appropriate measures to support a user's compliance requirements, the issue of inappropriate access still remains. What's to prevent an administrator at a provider from accessing a company's data? After all, administrators have access to the storage equipment the data resides on – remember, storage hardware is part of the infrastructure whose responsibility falls to the provider.

Providers recognise this issue and have addressed it. Most providers restrict access to infrastructure, implement role-based access control to ensure only appropriate personnel access infrastructure, log all access to infrastructure to ensure an audit trail, and regularly review those logs to find any inappropriate access events.

These measures are all appropriate, but they aren't foolproof. Tracking access is not the same as preventing access, and just as a company's own personnel may violate established processes, so, too, may a provider's.

For companies using a Cloud provider headquartered in the United States, an additional fillip is added to this issue. According to an article published in theregister.co.uk 4 July 2011, The US Patriot Act

gives law enforcement authorities the right to access personal data held by US-based companies, regardless of where it is stored in the world. The Act also gives law enforcers the right to prevent firms informing the customer that they have had to hand over the information. The controversial law was established as an anti-terrorism tool.

(*www.theregister.co.uk/2011/07/04/eu_customer_cloud_dat a_may_be_handed_over_by_microsoft/*)

In other words, as a user of a Cloud Computing service in the US, a user's data may be accessed by the US Federal Government, without any notice to the user that this access has occurred.

For many companies, the risk associated with possible data access by provider personnel, as well as the possible unacknowledged access by the US government, is too high.

The question then becomes, how can a Cloud user mitigate that risk while still enjoying the benefits of Cloud Computing?

Most companies in this circumstance turn to storage encryption. Encrypting data does not prevent access to the bits placed on a storage device. Encryption does, however, ensure that anyone lacking the decryption key, whether provider or US government personnel, cannot decipher the bits on the device to convert them back to their plaintext form. In other words, external users may have access to the storage device, but they lack the means to access meaningful information.

Of course, encrypting data means that the encryption key is supremely important. First, should the user lose the key, it would be impossible for the data to be accessed in a meaningful format. And don't assume that key loss could never happen in real life. It does.

Second, in order to prevent administrators and governmental employees from accessing the user's data, the keys must be stored in a place that no external party can access them

This implies that companies seeking to use encryption as a method of implementing data security must follow practices to keep decryption keys safe and protected from accidental loss. There are a number of commercial solutions available for key management and, of course, it's possible for a company to create its own secure key management solution. Whether a commercial or homegrown key management solution is implemented, handling keys safely and securely is extremely important.

Data security conclusion

The same caveats about the potential performance penalty of encryption noted in the section on network security apply to storage encryption as well. Rather than apply a blanket use of encryption, a better strategy is to assess which parts of the overall application data set are relevant from a security perspective and apply encryption to them. This requires judgement and, perhaps, additional engineering work to design the data schema and application itself to partition data into encrypted and unencrypted portions.

Notwithstanding the extra work, encryption is the only workable mechanism to truly ensure that data residing in a public Cloud environment is secure. Given the critical role data plays in today's business environment, ensuring its security is vital and encryption should be on every company's agenda when it comes to data security.

Instance security

Earlier in the chapter, we discussed how the assumptions underpinning traditional security approaches are no longer appropriate. The formerly stout wall represented by the perimeter of the data centre is now permeable – made so not by accident, but purposely by companies seeking to foster co-operation with external customers and partners.

When companies begin to use an external Cloud provider, the traditional security assumptions are even less appropriate. Common solutions to implement security – network-attached traffic monitors, centralised intrusion detection products and the like – cannot be installed in the multi-tenant resource pool implemented by Cloud providers. To address both the modified operational assumptions, as well as the shared resource environment, the phrase 'deperimeterisation of security' is used to indicate that the interior of a data centre is no longer a redoubt, safe from all external parties. Rather, the interior of a data centre is now a specialised location in which computing processes take place on behalf of users, but in which users have no direct control.

Consequently, rather than relying on centralised services to implement security practices, in a Cloud environment the scope of security is the instance. Each virtual machine in a user's application must have security practices present capable of providing security appropriate for the needs of the instance.

What then are the key elements of instance security? Here are six that should be addressed:

Firewall

Many providers place a firewall, either virtual or physical at the perimeter of a Cloud user's VLAN. The purpose of this firewall is to segregate traffic among all the users of the resource pool. However, the firewall being discussed in this chapter is not a perimeter-level firewall; rather it is a software firewall that resides within an instance itself.

The purpose of the instance-level firewall is to ensure that only traffic appropriate for the instance passes into the virtual machine. This means that only ports associated with the type of traffic the instance expects to receive and send are open. It may also mean that certain types of traffic are only accepted if they originate at a specific IP address.

Depending upon the Cloud provider and, indeed, the operating system of the instance, the configuration of the instance firewall may differ. No matter how the firewall is configured, however, setting the configuration properly to screen out unwanted traffic is very important. By definition, if traffic is unexpected, it is unwanted, and may also represent a threat. A firewall (as the name implies) is the first line of security for instance security and it is essential that it be operational and properly configured.

Configuring firewalls, particularly in Linux, can be challenging. If insufficient expertise is available in the user organisation, it is appropriate to contract with a firewall specialist to perform configuration. It should go without saying that, since application security resides above the trust boundary, correct configuration is the responsibility of the Cloud user and, should there be a security breakdown, the provider will abjure all responsibility.

System services

System services refer to utilities associated with an operating system. It is a general best practice, in all environments, whether Cloud or traditional, to only run necessary system services. All other system services should be configured to be inoperative while an instance is running.

This is a particularly important security measure, as a number of system services are notoriously vulnerable to attack. FTP, for example, has poor security and should not be running on a Cloud-deployed instance.

Limiting the number of system services running ensures that opportunities for attacks are minimised. Therefore, part of any application project should be defining which system services are required for every instance and ensuring that only those that are required run during instance operation.

Vulnerability assessment/penetration testing

This element of instance security evaluates how secure an instance is. It is not designed to prevent a security attack, but rather to help you harden your instances and prevent attacks. Vulnerability assessment refers to a process whereby an instance is scanned to evaluate if it has implemented appropriate security measures. For example, one aspect of vulnerability assessment would be to conduct a port scan to see if ports associated with unneeded system services are closed or not. A vulnerability assessment can be used to create a checklist of items to be addressed as part of a security hardening exercise.

Penetration testing goes a step further. It simulates an attack to identify vulnerabilities in operational systems. By mimicking an actual attack, this testing can help organisations characterise how their applications will withstand attempts to penetrate security and can help them modify applications to be more secure.

Performing this type of assessment and testing can be challenging in Cloud environments. Vulnerability testing commonly uses software installed within the data centre to scan machines; obviously in a controlled, shared environment, many Cloud providers are reluctant to allow this process to occur. There are vulnerability assessment services that operate from outside a data centre (i.e. they are SaaS offerings); they are more acceptable to Cloud providers, although they are limited in their ability to assess instances that may not have external IP addresses and, therefore, no way to reach them from outside the Cloud provider's environment.

Likewise, many Cloud providers frown on penetration testing, perhaps seeing it as little different from actual malicious attacks. Nevertheless, penetration testing is extremely useful and permission to perform penetration testing can usually be negotiated with a Cloud provider. Alternatively, the Cloud provider may have its own penetration testing team that can perform testing on your application.

However vulnerability assessment/penetration testing is performed, it should be part of your Cloud application security practices. Identifying vulnerabilities and addressing them can help protect your Cloud application.

Intrusion detection system/intrusion prevention system

These software products, commonly referred to as IDS/IPS refer to software installed on an instance to monitor instance activities and identify external intrusion events. These events are identified by comparing the events against policy definitions (e.g. three unsuccessful attempts to login as root within a five-minute period).

In the case of intrusion detection, the software response is to note the event and document it by placing an entry into a log. Monitoring log activity informs application administrators of inappropriate intrusion attempts and can provide information to help implement additional security measures.

Intrusion prevention goes a step further, as the name implies, to prevent intrusion by resetting the accessing party's network connection or creating a rule in the firewall to refuse traffic from the traffic source.

The type of intrusion detection used in a Cloud environment is referred to as HIDS, for host-based intrusion detection system, or HIPS, for, as you might guess, host-based intrusion prevention system.

There are a number of commercial and open source HIDS/HIPS products. Whichever type of software is used, it is critical that HIDS/HIPS be in place in a Cloud application. This is because the IP addresses associated with Cloud providers are well known and are constantly probed by malicious parties. Some have estimated that a new Cloud application is attacked less than 30 seconds after coming online.

Consequently, one must assume that malicious traffic will be directed at every Cloud application and HIDS/HIPS security should be implemented in every Cloud application instance. Users should also perform regular monitoring of the output of these systems as well to ensure awareness of traffic patterns, attack types, and so on, are understood.

Whatever HIDS/HIPS software is used, it should be updated immediately when new versions or new attack signatures are available.

Integrity checking/file change monitoring

Despite the best efforts of intrusion detection/prevention, it is possible that an intruder may gain access to an application instance in a manner that does not trigger an event alarm. This could result in the intruder modifying or replacing an instance file with one that contains code that executes something undesirable or dangerous. For example, a software file might be installed that tracks user logins as a way to capture user IDs and passwords.

One way to prevent this is to use security software that triggers an alert if a file is modified. This sort of software goes by several different names, including file integrity checking and file change monitoring. In fact, depending upon the product, this monitoring can go well beyond file monitoring and extend to database internals, Windows® registry entries and the like.

As one might expect, there are both commercial and open source products that provide this functionality.

Given the fact that Cloud-deployed applications are continuously under attack, implementing this element of instance security is fundamental to ensuring application security. Any change identified by an integrity checking product should be immediately addressed to remove the malicious code.

Anti-virus/anti-malware

For Windows® systems, anti-virus/anti-malware (AV/AM) software is necessary. Keeping malicious programs from being downloaded by users is vital to prevent application security problems. There are a plethora of AV/AM solutions available, both commercial and open source. Some of the commercial solutions are available at no charge.

AV/AM software should be part of the instance definition and not added later via installation by a system administrator. In other words, it should be part of the base system and operational from the moment the instance begins running. Furthermore, the signature files used by the AV/AM software should be updated immediately upon instance launch. There are a few solutions on the market that do not require signature file download because they use a Cloud-based approach to evaluate virus and malware presence. For Cloud-based applications, this can be a useful approach, given the fact that instances may be launched and terminated frequently; this Cloud-based approach avoids the overhead of repeatedly downloading the same signature file repeatedly.

Instance security conclusion

Instance security is perhaps the single most misunderstood aspect of Cloud security. Many organisations fail to address instance security in a methodical fashion. The reasons for this failing include:

- A misguided assumption that all responsibility for Cloud security falls on the provider. This book has repeatedly criticised that attitude, but it is commonly present in many Cloud users – at least until their first security breach when the Cloud provider points to the SLA and educates them about where application security responsibility lies.
- Lack of involvement by the IT security group. Many Cloud applications are being deployed by development groups, who select a Cloud-based deployment due to its ease and lack of organisation overhead. This overhead is perceived as delaying progress and, unfortunately, IT security groups are often considered an inconvenient overhead. Lacking sufficient security awareness, the application developers fail to implement appropriate practices, leaving the application vulnerable to attack.
- Lack of understanding how Cloud Computing characteristics affect security assumptions and practices. Many security practices are designed with an expectation that the computing environment will be stable, static and totally under the IT organisation's control and manually

configured. Cloud Computing, with its shared, dynamic, externally provided infrastructure clashes with those assumptions and can negate established security practices.

Whatever the reason for the failure to address instance security, Cloud users must change their security perspective and approach; they should follow practices that ensure appropriate security is implemented at the instance level. Only by doing so can the application be protected from penetration and attack.

Application architecture and deployment topology

A long-established best practice in application security is to partition the application topology, so that different tiers in the application are segregated from accessing one another directly.

The most common implementation of this approach is to install the web tier instances of an application on a different subnet from the database tier. Both tiers can communicate with the intervening tier, which is commonly an application server level. In this configuration, each tier's communication with another goes through a firewall; this ensures that only traffic for instances in the appropriate tier is forwarded, thereby enforcing tier segregation. Alternatively, VLANs can be used, which reduces the number of physical devices, but ensures logical separation of the tiers and enforces rules that ensure tier segregation.

In a Cloud environment, however, it is typically impossible to install physical firewalls in the environment. Users are commonly assigned a single VLAN for all the user's instances, no matter what type, tier or function.

This means that user solutions for application partitioning are not possible. Yet the need for application partitioning along tier lines is, if anything, more important in a shared Cloud environment. How can users implement tier segregation in a Cloud environment? Here are some commonly used techniques:

- *Evaluate additional providers* While many providers offer only single VLAN service to users, others can provide a firewall capable of defining and implementing subnets. This allows users to implement application topologies similar to what would be used in a corporate data centre. Widening one's search can locate providers who offer firewalls that support multiple subnets and thereby support desired application tier segregation.
- *Implement tier segregation at the instance firewall level* Each instance contains its own software firewall, and these can be configured to mimic VLAN or physical firewall segregation. Obviously, implementing this approach requires careful rule design and implementation, but it is possible, by its use, to achieve tier segregation.
- *Evaluate other Cloud provider mechanisms* Amazon has implemented what it refers to as security groups, which resemble software firewalls, but are defined and implemented at the account level, rather than at each software firewall. One can design security groups, so that adjacent tiers can communicate with one another while being unable to communicate with non-adjacent tiers. In fact, this can be taken one step further and different groups can be defined for each stage of the application life cycle, so that, for example, each stage's application has a web tier definition, but the definition is implemented such that a developer stage web tier

instance cannot communicate with a production stage application service instance. This approach can preclude accidental security breaches due to cross-stage instance communication.

No matter what approach one takes, it is appropriate to identify and implement an application topology design that prevents communication between tiers that should not have direct interaction. This represents a long-established best practice for application deployment. This also means that any attack that seeks to access the most critical asset – application data – must hop across multiple instances to gain data access. In other words, even if an attack gains access to a web tier instance, before it can gain access to the storage (database) tier, it must first gain access and successfully attack the intervening application server tier.

Application architecture and deployment topology conclusion

Implementing and enforcing application tier segregation as part of an application topology is important, so much so that it is established as a widely accepted best practice.

The usual mechanisms to achieve tier segregation are usually not available in a Cloud environment. There are other methods to achieve the same results, though, and organisations implementing Cloud applications should definitely take advantage of them.

Tier segregation makes security breaches more difficult to execute and reduces the potential for loss and, therefore, risk. Evaluation of how to achieve tier segregation within the target Cloud environment should be part of every Cloud application's design and project plan.

Code update and patch management

The chapter thus far has addressed how to make an application secure against external attacks. It is clear that consistent application of best practices, modified as needed to address the characteristics of operating in a shared Cloud environment, is a prerequisite for achieving appropriate security. For example, we discussed how to use intrusion detection and prevention to block attacks.

How does one make sure, though, that the application itself has all appropriate security measures in place? Software components are constantly updated with patches to address security vulnerabilities. Unquestionably, operating an application in a Cloud environment necessitates the consistent and rapid application of patches to instances running in the Cloud.

A common practice in Cloud environments is to mirror practices followed in corporate data centres. This is to create a template of the full instance image – operating system, middleware and application software – and use that as the basis to launch instances. Certainly, this approach is better than the alternative – launching a bare virtual machine, and installing and configuring all software components by hand. Is it the best approach for a Cloud environment, though?

The drawback to this approach is that the entire image must be re-created every time a single patch is applied. This inevitably leads to what is referred to as 'image sprawl', where multiple similar images (but each with small variations) exist. The situation is tailor-made for confusion and lack of transparency about what a running application is comprised of – does it have image 123a or 123b? The potential for chaos is obvious. Worse still, the potential that important patches are not applied across all images that are running could be catastrophic.

Most of the most sophisticated Cloud users – the so-called 'webscale' applications like Netflix and the like – follow a different approach to image management. Rather than creating a master image with all necessary software components in it, instead they begin with a 'bare bones' image that only has the smallest necessary parts of the operating system in it.

When an instance is launched, a separate definition is consulted that outlines what middleware and application software components are required to execute the role the instance will perform. Those components are dynamically and automatically installed in the bare bones image; once the image is complete, with all the necessary software components installed and operating, the instance is moved into production as a part of the application topology.

Typically, the installed software components are drawn directly from the configuration management system in which they are stored.

The benefit of this 'dynamic construction' approach is that security patches are applied in only one place – the software component version stored in the configuration management system – but are automatically deployed every time that software component is required for a particular instance type.

In addition, rather than having image sprawl (many versions of full image templates exist) and someone having to keep track of which is the right image and ensure it is launched, this approach centralises the image definitions, ensuring that launching the right version is easily accomplished.

Furthermore, updating the instances in a running application is simple: a running instance is terminated, and when it is subsequently re-launched it automatically picks up the latest version with the correct patches applied.

The basis of this approach is simplification of process and consistency of administration through automation. Avoiding human intervention and reducing manual tasks reduces the potential for mistakes. Security patches and code changes only have to be applied once, and all subsequent instance launches automatically pick up the right version of software components.

Naturally, this process modification requires effort and a change in operations. Co-operation between application developers and the operations groups that administer applications while in production needs to be far closer than in traditional environments. The differences between this approach and the traditional methods of application operations are significant enough that the new approach has been christened with its own name: DevOps.

Code update and patch management conclusion

It does little good to implement elaborate application protection mechanisms when the application itself is insecure due to outdated or vulnerable code. Organisations seeking to operate Cloud applications must follow practices designed to ensure all necessary code changes and security patches are applied, and only instances containing those changes and patches are put into production.

The most sophisticated and experienced Cloud application do not follow the established mechanisms of launching instances based on full image templates. Instead, they use a common foundation for all instances consisting of a bare bones operating system, into which required software components are dynamically installed. This enforces consistency and reduces the potential for confusion. Critically, it makes them more certain that important security patches are applied and put into production.

Those organisations seeking to gain the most from Cloud Computing should emulate the webscale companies and follow their best practices. Doing so will help increase overall application security and reduce risk.

Conclusion

This has been a lengthy chapter, which should illustrate a core truth of Cloud Computing: even when using a Cloud provider, users retain significant responsibility for the overall security of their systems. While the provider must – by definition – implement security for those aspects of the overall environment that are not controlled by the Cloud user, that does not absolve the user from all responsibility for security.

Any elements of the total solution that reside above the trust boundary fall under the user's control, and security of those aspects of the solution is the user's responsibility. Many organisations fail to recognise this fact, and suffer when incomplete or missing security elements expose their users or data to security breaches.

Once the user's responsibility for security above the trust boundary is acknowledged, it's not sufficient to transfer existing security practices from the user's own data centre into the Cloud provider's environment.

While most internal data centres can rely on security practices that assume stable and static environments that are dedicated to a single user organisation, Cloud Computing environments do not support such an assumption. Instead, Cloud users must recognise that their security measures must be implemented in a manner appropriate for a shared, dynamic and elastic environment. This typically requires a major rethink of security assumptions and practices.

This chapter has outlined a number of areas that are subject to that rethink process and has offered recommendations to assist the reader in understanding what changes need to be made to areas that lie above the trust boundary. Following these recommendations should provide a good basis for application security. We recommend, however, that all Cloud users revisit and re-evaluate their application security measures; the constantly evolving nature of Cloud Computing means that new solutions and approaches are likely to be available to further improve Cloud application security.

CHAPTER 7: ORGANISATIONAL RISKS ASSOCIATED WITH CLOUD COMPUTING

Organisational risks are threats, negative effects or problems due to internal or external changes in organisational structure or management processes that can impact the mission of a company or an organisation. While many organisations practise operational risk management, few practise organisational risk management although they are intimately tied together. An organisation operates through the combination of people, processes and technology working together. If any one of these categories has a major structural impact, it will most likely affect the other two categories.

One of the major sources of organisational risk is the introduction of new technologies. In an exceptional example of the domino effect, new technologies tend to bring about changes in processes, which in turn impact the individuals who are implementing those processes today. Some technologies are more disruptive than others. Disruptive changes can force entire shifts in personnel and management.

Cloud Computing has the potential to be extremely disruptive for business in general, but significantly for information technology departments. Over the years, IT had few choices with regard to delivery of information services. Typically, the options were either build it yourself, outsource it completely, or some combination thereof. Regardless, the existing options were expensive. In due course, prices of commodity computing hardware dropped and availability of reliable high-speed networking increased, enabling new, competitively priced options to appear on the market offering users another option for delivery of information services.

As organisations adopt Cloud Computing, the domino effect will ensue and existing processes will need to change, which will drive changes in personnel requirements. This is a major organisational risk and one that has the potential to severely impair an organisation, if it is not addressed as part of the adoption planning.

Organisational risks of Cloud Computing

With regard to Cloud Computing, there is consensus among IT professionals that at some point in their career they are going to have to make a decision with regard to the use of Cloud Computing. This decision may be due to the emphasis being placed on it in the press and media, the ramblings of their internal management looking to cut IT costs and hastily jumping to the conclusion that Cloud Computing will provide that for them, or because they themselves want to gain familiarity with emerging technologies to keep their skills up to date and, hence, keep themselves marketable. Notice, none of these reasons represents Cloud Computing as better, faster or cheaper than current solutions.

The last paragraph illustrates why avoiding the Cloud Computing disruption may be very difficult, if not impossible. As Larry Ellison, Oracle founder and CEO, has been quoted in the press as saying: 'The IT industry is more fashion-driven than the women's fashion industry.' That is to say that IT professionals are sometimes more taken with what is 'hot' than what makes more sense for their business. When coupled with the speed of change that we see in technology industry, this makes it very difficult to undertake projects that last longer than a year or two without incurring some disruptive event.

Hence, we can assume that Cloud Computing will be adopted in some way, shape or form within most organisations within the next five years. The reason that Cloud Computing represents an organisational risk is that it changes where and how resources are applied. This means financial, human and computing resources will be employed differently than they are now, which is typically followed by fear and concern. Unmanaged, that fear and concern will shape your organisation in potentially negative ways. Thus, executives and IT leadership must get in front of this coming disruption and plan accordingly.

Here's a list of some of the ways that Cloud Computing will change how resources are applied:

- You may decide not to continue managing your own data centre, but instead acquire Cloud-based solutions.
- You may realise that you need new personnel to leverage the emerging solutions, such as analytics and disaster recovery.
- You may decide that it's now easier for some of your workforce to telecommute and organise accordingly.
- You may decide that certain field offices are no longer necessary and decide to close them.

Much like a chess game, each of these decisions, as well as the many not listed here, will impact your organisation, your personnel, your vendors and your customers. Thus, executives and IT leadership should be asking themselves the following questions today:

- Is my organisation ready for Cloud Computing?
- Is Cloud Computing better than what I'm currently using? If so, why?
- Will my staff be concerned that I will downsize after moving to the Cloud?
- How should I incorporate Cloud Computing into my business?
- How will using Cloud Computing change how I manage the use of IT in my business?
- What will Cloud Computing allow me to do that I couldn't do before?
- What will Cloud Computing allow me to do more cost-effectively?
- Which service model is right for my business?
- Which deployment model is right for my business?

Additionally, while these are good questions and appropriate for various representatives of the business to be asking, they will require first going through the exercise of defining the future goals of the business, identifying the demand forecast for IT infrastructure and services, and specifying business requirements that would justify the use of Cloud Computing. In essence, the choice for Cloud Computing is directly related to your business strategy and/or mission. And, anything that impacts your business strategy/mission is guaranteed to be an organisational risk.

Cloud Computing does and doesn't change everything

If it is viewed as a means of outsourcing management and operation of your IT infrastructure and platforms, Cloud Computing can be a paradigm shift for your organisation.

That is, Cloud Computing does represent the opportunity to rethink the past 30 years of organic growth within IT. While many significant changes occurred over the past 30 years, key information systems were primarily created, managed and serviced by an internal organisation using internal resources. Some very large organisations were successfully outsourcing management of their infrastructure and support at various points during that period,[3] but overall many organisations built their own, in some cases duplicative,[4] infrastructure. Using Cloud Computing as a means of delivering the same or greater service using more productive and cost-effective means represents a strong organisational risk.

Cloud Computing can also be viewed simply as an effective means of utilising computing resources, which may require some retraining or new hires to operationally support, but does not change the way the business views IT or its role in the organisation. Thus, Cloud Computing can simply be leveraged as a tool for some levels of greater efficiencies without significantly changing processes and personnel.

Ultimately, the way in which Cloud Computing is embraced by the organisation plays a significant role in the downstream impact of the choice to use Cloud Computing. Some organisations embrace change, while others respond negatively – especially where fiefdoms have formed. Ignoring organisational risk management has allowed

---

[3] *www.cioinsight.com/c/a/Case-Studies/GM-Outsourcing-Overhaul-1-Year-Later/*

[4] *http://www.cio.gov/documents/State-of-the-Federal-Datacenter-Consolidation-Initiative-Report.pdf*

various actors within an organisation to amass unhealthy levels of power and control. Threats to that power base can result in unprecedented disruption to the business. In many cases, Cloud Computing represents a threat to these individuals' sense of security and control over the organisation.

There are some aspects of Cloud Computing that impinge heavily on closely held IT environments. For example, migrating applications to a public Cloud means that there is less of a need for the same quantity of infrastructure to be managed internally. This is in direct conflict with the sense of ownership and job security associated with having built and managing a large quantity of infrastructure. Hence, moving to public Cloud Computing can be deemed as a loss of power and vulnerability for the staff currently managing operations. Reactions can range from a general reduction in the quality of service due to apathy and concern to vengeful responses that demonstrate what a critical role these individuals play.

When the threat is perceived by the CIO, the effects can even be more difficult to identify. The CIO may perceive Cloud Computing as a business threat, as well as a personal threat. Regardless, how they respond may be indistinguishable from the cause. The CIO may state their recommendation against Cloud Computing is that they cannot ensure that the customer is properly supported or that it has the potential to negatively impact mission-critical systems. Either way, these are difficult cases to debate as there is an aspect of truth to them.

Overcoming the objections of those reacting out of fear and being threatened by those that hide behind a curtain of fear, uncertainty and doubt is both an operational and organisational risk for the business. However, there are ways to chip away at this perception without driving a major confrontation.

Consider the following scenario:

An enterprise development team developing a single distributed application may require anywhere from three to ten servers to model a production environment. Since operations is required to manage the use and tracking of licences, as well as set up and tear down of development environments in the data centre, the request to configure this many servers may have sat idle waiting while the IT team satisfies production requests first. Moreover, it is possible that the IT group may respond to this request by applying an artificial limitation on how many servers development is actually allowed without any logical or financial reason.

As a result, the development manager decides to utilise a public Cloud Computing service that charges only for the time, storage and bandwidth. While using this service results in unexpected expenses for the development team, the development manager can make the case that they waited for IT, the request took too long or was insufficient for development to complete their tasks and meet their deadlines. So, for a nominal charge, the development manager was able to identify an alternative solution and achieve the business goals.

This can happen in organisations where individuals are empowered to take responsibility for meeting agreed7 goals and milestones. Thus, part of managing organisational risk is to empower individuals to find cost-effective ways to solve problems. In this case, doing so also has the potential to lead to the following outcomes:

- illustrates IT as being ineffective in supporting the needs of development with regard to meeting objectives and timelines;
- raises questions whether internal infrastructure should be used for internal development given there are cost-

effective ways to support development without impacting operations and using expensive resources;

* illustrates a path for lowering operational costs in the future;
* rethinking how budget for IT is allocated.

With Cloud Computing now an option, the CIO has to consider the impact to the overall IT budget and the politics associated with attempting to hinder Cloud Computing as an alternative. Either the CIO must become more responsive to requests for resource allocation or suffer the consequences that resources will be acquired through Cloud service providers. Regardless, it makes it much more difficult for individuals to operate out of fear and continue to support their decisions.

Here's another common scenario that businesses are starting to see with regard to availability of Cloud-based solutions.

The sales team is consistently complaining that they cannot access the sales force enablement application when they are on the road, leading to long lags until the information is updated in the system. This makes it very difficult for sales and marketing management to track the success of the various sales programs. The VP of sales finally makes a decision to use a SaaS-based customer relationship management system, which the sales team has used in a small field trial with great success.

The CIO and chief information security officer (CISO) push back against the use of SaaS arguing that using publicly available services may be too risky if not configured and integrated properly. However, when asked how long it would take to overcome these issues, the CIO responds that it will take at least two to three months. The decision of the CEO is to accept the risk and acquire the SaaS-based solution.

With the business focused on revenue generation and growth for the company, alternatives like this may seem mission critical and move forward without the co-operation of IT. Time to market for deploying these solutions make them very attractive to business executives. Moreover, when compared to their experiences deploying these solutions in house, SaaS solutions are seemingly simpler.

Today's SaaS environments are highly configurable, but tend to stop short of being fully programmable. This configurability is what makes them so powerful and a reason for their popularity. Since each organisation has their own processes and methods of doing things, SaaS applications can allow a function, such as customer relationship management, sales force management and accounting, to be retrofitted to the needs of the business. However, SaaS configurability limits the number of things that can be configured, which, interestingly, has a positive effect on the outcome. This is understandable when compared to an internal IT organisation customising an expensive software application or developing it from scratch; the expectation is to deliver every possible combination that the business desires.

From an organisational risk perspective, this sense of rapid responsiveness and success associated with easy access and simple SaaS configurability often has an associated effect of making IT seem ineffective and unresponsive. This is one of those cases where Cloud Computing's greatest strengths is also its greatest weakness. Cloud Computing is designed to be on-demand and self-service, but service providers do not have the added responsibility for ensuring that your data is accessible by other departments and applications within the organisation. Moreover, they may actually have limits on how data is accessed and may charge differently based upon which access methods are used. Ultimately, it falls on IT to figure out how to ensure this data is shared, integrated and made available.

In the end, ignoring organisational risk due to adoption of Cloud Computing can lead to one or more of the following:

- Business unit leaders may replicate IT functionality within their own group.
- Mission-critical data is vulnerable and not well integrated into existing business processes.
- Access to corporate data may result in unplanned or higher-than-expected costs.

Impact of Cloud Computing on executive decision-making roles

Ultimately, the major shift in Cloud Computing is not a technical one, but an economic one. Cloud Computing enables a level of agility that previously was possible, but had a very high cost. This shift is being recognised by business leaders and executives and is having a profound impact on their thinking about IT investments.

The following section explores some of the considerations that various C-level executives are currently facing that Cloud Computing can help with, or that they should be considering because of the availability of Cloud Computing solutions.

Executive team

Contrary to belief, the decision to adopt Cloud Computing may not be solely a capital expenditure and/or IT decision. Cloud Computing challenges many of the commonly held beliefs about what is achievable and the timeframes for achieving them within information technology.

Prior to the general availability of certain Cloud Computing solutions, it would have taken considerable financial and human resources to combine all of the businesses' sales and marketing data into a single repository and develop analytics that help to visualise critical patterns within that data. Today, this problem can be solved in anywhere from one week to ten hours at a hundredth the cost, leveraging a combination of public Cloud Computing services and new data management tools, such as Hadoop. For this reason, Cloud Computing is a game changer that is worthy of the entire executive team's attention.

Adopting Cloud Computing will impact internal business processes. For businesses that have invested in Capability Maturity Model Integration (CMMI)®, ISO20000, ISO27000 or are undergoing internal business process management (BPM) efforts, there will be associated costs to update and qualify changes due to adoption of Cloud Computing. Whether integrating the Cloud into your existing environment, such as you would in a hybrid deployment model, or if you migrate to a public Cloud deployment model, your internal business processes are most likely going to be affected. Moreover, these processes will impact multiple departments, and the executive team will need to analyse, as a group, the costs and time associated with these modifications.

There is a considerable risk for the business in not analysing and understanding process change costs prior to adoption, as they can have a major impact on the business in the form of lost opportunities due to other tasks not being addressed, requirement for additional labour and reprioritisation of other initiatives. Additionally, it is not just IT resources that will be required to participate in these process changes, so all stakeholders need to understand how their business areas will be impacted.

CEO/COO

At this point in time, it is a widely accepted belief that information technology provides businesses with market advantages. While the CEO/COO must be capable of fully understanding the impact of IT decisions, they don't need to understand the esoteric issues related to how Cloud services operate; but they should understand the value proposition for Cloud Computing, the risks associated with various service and deployment models, and the financial impact to their business.

Successfully adopting Cloud Computing may require the co-operation of multiple facets of the business, including human resources, finance, legal, accounting, in addition to IT. Hence, the CEO needs to facilitate the critical conversations and establish the priorities for working together to be able to take advantage of the benefits of Cloud Computing. Human resources needs to analyse the impact of Cloud Computing on their current skills matrix and how adoption may be perceived by and impact current IT workers. CEOs should also work with their legal team to understand the ramifications for the business with regard to their relationship with their customers, board, banks, credit card merchants, government and so on. The decision to use public Cloud services may impact certain businesses more than others due to factors related to their affiliations and accreditation, as well as the need to remain compliant with industry and government regulations. Finally, CEOs will want to issue appropriate policies for the acquisition of these services on behalf of the business, so that business units do not accidentally replicate services unnecessarily.

CIO

The CIO has perhaps the most difficult role with regard to adoption of Cloud Computing. They need to balance the interest of the business against the rising costs of IT operations and spending. At a time where a major percentage of the IT budget is spent on 'keeping the lights on', they must act as the gatekeeper and pragmatist over a major economical shift with regard to IT spending. In addition to these functions, they will be constantly faced with a growing need for speed and a backlog of requests for new functionality and capabilities. Moreover, they will feel the pressure by the business to shift to Cloud-based services on anecdotal successes of industry peers.

Managing through these competing interests is going to require a considerable amount of effort by the CIO to educate the business on the situation. Attempting to juggle these balls by themselves is a recipe for disaster. The next generation of CIOs need to be able to lead, not manage. They need to engage the other business leaders in understanding and solving the entire problem domain. They need to make their peers understand the implications and risks the organisation will face making certain choices, such as selecting SaaS solutions versus spending on private Cloud equivalents.

CFO

The CFO needs to understand how the organisation's current investment in underutilised compute resources impacts overall IT spending requirements. In addition, they need to gain deeper understanding of how various Cloud Computing solutions can provide alternatives to consistently accumulating and operating more and more infrastructure.

Questions the CFO should seek to answer for the business includes:

- Will the business need to continue to add hardware to support one application while significant hardware investments go underutilised in the data centre?
- Is the demand for more hardware an attempt to meet peak operating demand versus average operating demand?
- Is the business paying for software licences that it doesn't use or could phase out through alternative solutions?

Most CFOs never dreamed that once they completed their general accounting education, they would need to also become versed in information technology. And they don't. Clearly, there are plenty of individuals who are versed in accounting and financial management that also understand technology. These individuals should hold a role in the CFO's office and be responsible for data centre and IT financial modelling and analysis. The key point here is if the business is investing millions of dollars in information technology, it's a tiny additional overhead to hire someone who can ensure that the technical approach and the financial investment are aligned.

One of the most critical analyses that will be facing CFOs shortly will be to fund use of public or private Cloud. The difficult thing about this decision is that is has both technical and financial components that must be balanced. The CFO will have to prioritise risk, which may or may not be able to be quantified and may only be able to be supported through anecdotal evidence, against capital expenditure and cash flow. Or simply stated, does it make sense for my business to enter into a long-term subscription with a Cloud service provider versus building this infrastructure internally? Note, in this scenario, we include private external and virtual private Cloud into the public bucket because from a financial standpoint the key factor will be accepting the risk associated accepting long-term operational expenditure and the associated costs as a replacement for the assets and overhead associated with ownership.

CTO

Due to the many variations of the role of the CTO, we will focus on CTOs that help to identify and select technologies that will meet the business requirements and future demand. In a well-oiled executive team, the CTO and CIO work hand in hand. The CIO is collecting and prioritising the business requirements and handing them off to the CTO to seek out technology solutions. While the CIO is focused on governance, the CTO is identifying solutions that will operate within the CIOs governance framework. When the CTO identifies a technology, such as Cloud Computing, that impacts the CIO's governance model, the CTO is the one that should provide the adoption roadmap.

This approach works well when there's trust and mutual respect between the CTO and CIO, but that is not always the case. When there is distrust between the CTO and CIO or simply a philosophical difference in the way they believe the enterprise needs to go technologically, there can be a significant disruption in the business. Cloud Computing represents a possibly challenging condition for this relationship. To state it bluntly, Cloud has the ability to shift power in the direction of either the CIO or CTO depending upon what value is associated with Cloud adoption. If the business perceives Cloud Computing as purely technological, the CTO's responsibility could increase significantly relative to those of the CIO. If the business perceives Cloud Computing as an economical value, then the CTO's position may be jeopardised or greatly minimised.

Impact of Cloud Computing on traditional IT roles

By default, Cloud Computing does not require an IT department to change its processes or modify its skills set. The fact that the change occurs is in response to the types of changes that Cloud Computing enables. For example, many IT organisations are vastly underdeveloped in their disaster recovery (DR) and continuity of operations (COOP) planning and support due to the high costs associated with reducing the recovery time and point objectives. Prior to Cloud alternatives, the closer an organisation came to 100% uptime, the more expensive the solution. Thus, businesses settled for 'acceptable' recovery time and point objectives, where acceptable represented anywhere from one day to one week, depending upon management's appetite for pain versus expense.

Today's Cloud Computing options significantly lower the costs and complexity associated with reducing recovery time and point objectives. For a nominal monthly charge, businesses can produce cold and warm back-up sites that can become operational in hours without the overhead of keeping a completely separate co-location facility or secondary data centre. Moreover, the virtualisation technologies used in many Cloud Computing solutions facilitate rapid failover to the Cloud Computing site. It is relatively easy for an organisation to add this DR/COOP capability to their existing environment without major modifications. However, most IT organisations will receive greater benefits if they take the opportunity to re-think their current approach and processes and add the appropriate resources needed to create a more resilient environment.

In some cases, Cloud Computing will drive significant changes in organisational structure and resource allocation. For example, businesses looking to Cloud Computing for purposes of lowering operational IT costs by replacing on-premises managed hardware with Infrastructure-as-a-Service (IaaS), will most likely see reductions in labour as well as capital expenditures. In this particular scenario, engineers responsible for managing the power, cooling, racking and other general data centre maintenance jobs would no longer be required; at least not by the Cloud service consumers.

Here are a list of some traditional IT roles and how they might be impacted by the adoption of Cloud Computing:

- *System administrators*   SysAdmins play a critical role in the management of platforms and systems located on premises or acquired as a service. In a Cloud Computing environment, SysAdmins are also expected to develop and use automation tools more effectively, which includes having the ability to develop complex scripts and programs. They may also find that they are required to have a greater understanding of multiple operating system platforms in contrast to today, where operating systems is an area of specialisation.

- *Network administrators* The role of the NetAdmin is uncertain with the introduction of Cloud Computing. On perspective, a move to a public infrastructure could mean that fewer NetAdmins are required since most of the critical network installation, configuration and maintenance will be handled by the Cloud service provider. The converse is also possible given that the Cloud can contain an unlimited number of virtual networks; there may be a need for more NetAdmins since building these networks out is no longer constrained physically. Regardless, where the NetAdmin does their work and the type of appliance they are working on will change, but, ultimately, they will still be managing switches, routers and firewalls.

- *Software engineers* Due to the growing trend to leverage inexpensive storage, memory and bandwidth, software engineers have formulated bad habits of treating these components as infinite. The result of this behaviour is that some applications are now much more difficult to migrate to the Cloud. Applications that made assumptions about network latency, memory sizes, disk I/O speeds and processor capabilities may find that these assumptions do not hold in a multi-tenant environment like the Cloud. Thus, Cloud Computing may require software engineers to carefully consider their designs and how they are utilise compute resources, so that they operate as good neighbours in a multi-tenant environment.

- *Storage engineers* Storage engineers' skills are oriented towards managing demand versus capacity and designing for use. Thus, for businesses moving to IaaS there will be little need for storage engineers as long as the SysAdmins and software engineers have a good grasp on how the IaaS storage options will impact application execution. In hybrid Cloud environments, businesses that have unique data management issues will still continue with strong demand for storage engineers. For example, business that manage large volumes of media or need to capture multiple streams of data being received at very high speeds will need to consider how best to store that data for responsive retrieval and growth. In the private Cloud environment, the storage engineer is very critical since the storage area network (SAN) is essentially the lifeblood of the private Cloud. Proper partitioning of disk arrays, redundancy architectures and demand management will make or break a Cloud environment.
- *Security engineers* Security engineers base their experience on understanding the body of knowledge associated with industry best practices and standards versus a single environment. Thus, the security engineer's experience and knowledge will need to support multiple Cloud Computing architectures. Due to the newness and rapid advancement, there are threats associated with Cloud Computing that may take even the most senior security engineers by surprise because they lack the full understanding of the Cloud implementation and because there may be components that are now outside of their control. Hence, Cloud Computing does

require security engineers to get up to speed more quickly than some of the other IT roles discussed here. This also means that, for some, the Cloud is inherently more risky until this education and experience problem is overcome.

- *Data centre operator* Cloud Computing, in any deployment model, lowers the total complexity of managing the data centre and should result in a need for fewer operators. Moreover, with a focus on automation, human operator involvement in problem resolution will become less and less of a requirement. Hence, it may be a good idea to retrain some of these operators to assist in other areas of IT service management, such as the help desk.

- *Architects* With the rise in interest in Cloud Computing comes a greater need for high-quality Cloud architects. Being a new paradigm, albeit one that is closely related to other similar design paradigms, means there are not enough trained architects that understand the nuances for building, supporting and designing for the Cloud. For years, the industry focus has been on distancing the software architects from needing to understand the underlying hardware platforms on which their applications would execute. Meanwhile, data centre architects have been focusing on virtualisation and networking without really focusing on what's running on these virtualised environments. It is the Cloud architect's role to liaise between these two areas of specialisation and to consider the ramifications of each to produce a design that will meet the business's requirements.

Instituting DevOps

While there are changes on the horizon for IT roles due to adoption of Cloud Computing, the change that organisations need to pay heed to is the DevOps movement. DevOps is the growing organisational trend that integrates development, operations and QA into a collaborative delivery unit to improve quality and performance.

Today's IT organisations are typically organised around specialisation of knowledge. Roles are organised in silos oriented around specific components of the IT organisation. Individuals have specialisations in networking, servers, storage, virtualisation, operating systems and desktops, and software development. Due to economic trends to reduce IT overhead and technological advances from convergence of technologies into a single platform, in the future, silos will be broken up and individuals will focus on the system rather than components.

This means that there will be fewer positions and those positions will be held by individuals that have a generalisation in multiple technologies. They will be able to configure and operate an entire Cloud architecture that consists of networking, servers and storage. Moreover, they will have programming skills that enable them to implement automation controls over this environment, allowing them to do more with fewer resources.

In the past, where development was done in a specialised development environment that was utopian compared to the operational environment it will run in, development will be done in the actual runtime environment. Applications will be developed as a set of services in the Cloud that can only be tested under real-world conditions. There will be a greater focus on unit testing as a means of ensuring quality with an understanding that changes may need to be rolled back to a previous version quickly. Furthermore, developers will be an active participant in the roll-out and maintenance of the service in production. This is the basis for the DevOps movement.

DevOps has been defined as a movement, a role and a way of life. Admittedly, those who see DevOps as a way of life are those deeply involved in performing tasks associated with DevOps. The point is that DevOps is not concretely defined or agreed upon by the industry, yet it is playing a critical role in the restructuring of IT operations. It's also a key factor in evolving quality in IT organisations, which has an overall impact of lowering organisational risk.

For the purposes of this book, we will define DevOps as a framework or organisational structure that enables IT organisations to deliver with greater quality and more agility. DevOps is a form of service development/delivery life cycle (SDLC) that leverages approaches and processes from agile software development that incorporates involvement from quality assurance and operations throughout the entire life cycle. This early collaboration results in some key benefits and lowers overall risk:

- Quality assurance and operations are more informed about the use of the application from the end-user perspective and have a better understanding of the end-user. Through this information, the operations team is far more capable of handling production issues as they arise.
- Quality assurance and operations have a better understanding of the mechanics of the application, which allows them to deliver better support throughout testing and production.

- Software development gains insight early enough into the project related to potential production-level problems and can design around those issues.
- Problem resolution is faster and more effective as there is less finger pointing and there is an established means of collaboration between everyone as a team.

DevOps is not a new concept, but very rarely implemented by mid- and large-sized businesses. Indeed, the larger the organisation the less likely it will be for development and operations to communicate regularly. Anecdotally, it has been observed that in many large IT organisations, operations spends an inordinate amount of time correcting and handling issues that arise in production due to faulty or buggy software. Yet, very rarely is a member of development part of the team responsible for restoring service without executive-level intervention due to escalation and significant customer impact.

With recent advancements in operations automation, due in part to a focus on Cloud Computing, which boasts self-service as one of its attributes, DevOps has really garnered more industry attention. This is due to the raised awareness that SysAdmins can now develop scripts that simplify the maintenance and operation of a virtualised environment.

Application programming interfaces (API) provided by the vendors of virtualisation software allows SysAdmins to significantly control how a virtualised machine operates. Through these APIs they can control memory allocation, starting and stopping, where the virtualised machine is running, how many instances of a certain machine are running (used for load-balancing), and they can dynamically change the personality of the machine (e.g. IP addresses, routing and so on). SysAdmins that have learned how to program to leverage these APIs are very much in demand.

However, in less mature organisations this skill has been confused with software engineering, and thus, the organisation attempts to build their DevOps base using enterprise application developers. This is a significant organisational risk related to Cloud Computing. SysAdmins don't want to develop applications and application developers do not want to administer infrastructure.

Hence, one of the key risks with regard to the success of a DevOps programme is the introduction of the concept to upper management. In businesses where DevOps was introduced as a role instead of a process or framework, management associated the position with an opportunity to reduce headcount: upper management believed that they could hire a team of DevOps one-third the size of their current staff to handle the SDLC. Moreover, once the concept was introduced in this manner, it became a significant hurdle to redefine the effort as a process or a framework.

One additional note regarding DevOps and auditing: the separation between development and operations we discussed at the beginning of the chapter has sometimes been seen as an advantage by auditors, as it acts to limit certain risks, such as breaking of security controls. Moving to DevOps doesn't necessitate the breakdown of this separation completely, but in certain cases, depending upon how it's implemented, the DevOps concept can act to facilitate the introduction of software artefacts into production that may have previously been caught. Related to the prior note about management using DevOps as an opportunity to consolidate development and operations under a single individual or group of individuals, this risk may increase significantly and supports the earlier point that this is an inappropriate way to conceive a DevOps organisation.

Developing for a multi-tenant universe

Multi-tenancy, which is an important facet of Cloud Computing, will challenge behaviours of your organisation's developers that have been building enterprise software under the guise of having full access to all resources of the entire platform. This may require you to consider the costs and time implications associated with training, as well as a possible need for new hires that understand developing for a Cloud environment.

Even though virtualisation has been rampantly changing the landscape of the data centre, these changes have not been fully incorporated into and adopted by the software development group. Enterprise applications developed as recently as last year may have been developed on dedicated server platforms: the databases, application servers, web servers and other components all run on dedicated hardware in the development environment. Due to this configuration, developers do not witness performance issues that the application may suffer in a virtual production environment. This often leads to operations spending inordinate amounts of time struggling to alleviate performance issues and getting these applications to operate properly in a virtual environment. Indeed, a popular response that has been satirised with regard to this effect is: 'It worked in the test environment!'

The problem and associated risks arise because the multi-tenant environment shares physical resources in a way that the dedicated hardware does not. Applications running on the same physical server but in virtualised server instances will all be using the same physical network adapters, memory bus and storage connectors. Hypervisors will do their best to throttle and deliver quality of service to each machine instance, but there's still the opportunity for one process to starve the others. If the developers do not stress test their application in this environment, co-located with the other applications that it will be running with in production, there is the potential that the application will not perform.

This issue also demonstrates the increased complexity associated with managing a Cloud Computing environment. Cloud administrators must be aware of how resources are being consumed and be prepared to separate processes that are not well-suited to co-exist on the same physical servers. Good Cloud management software will enable these rules to be created as policies, thus simplifying the problem, but every time a new application is introduced into the Cloud environment, the risk of a clash between the new and existing applications is possible.

The runaway train: Cloud sprawl

The fact that Cloud Computing enables business to acquire Cloud services with the swipe of a credit card means that Cloud sprawl represents a significant organisational risk. Not only does Cloud sprawl introduce unexpected and unplanned expenses, these expenses may represent redundancy of data and applications. Moreover, Cloud sprawl undermines the ability of the CIO and CISO to ensure that the organisation's data is properly managed and protected.

In the early days of personal computing, IT was faced with a daunting problem that they were unprepared to handle – PC sprawl. Prior to personal computers, desktop support meant replacing the terminal with a new one. However, the business was always tethered to the glass house, which meant that IT controlled the environment. With the advent of personal computers, business leaders could use their own budget to acquire equipment and run PC applications locally without the permission or controls of IT. Ultimately, it took IT a decade to put that genie back in its bottle. Now, a new genie has arrived and a similar scenario to the personal computer sprawl is possible.

Once IT got the personal computer sprawl under control, many IT organisations made the mistake of returning to old glass-house habits: they didn't treat the business like customers. The result was that the business was constantly frustrated by the lack of IT support and consistently looking for alternate solutions whenever possible. Enter Cloud Computing and the ability for the business to acquire IT services using their own budget and it's the making for a repeat of the PC sprawl scenario all over again. This is exactly what is occurring in many organisations worldwide.

The risk for the business this time is that Cloud Computing solutions constrain the business from implementing many of the controls and processes it developed over the years to protect its data and ensure its availability. So, when the business chooses to start using a new SaaS application or they hire external developers who put their application in a PaaS without including IT in the decision, the business's data is at risk. This is not a criticism of the security risk associated with Cloud Computing; that will be covered elsewhere in this book. This risk is a symptom of these new applications existing outside the business's disaster recovery and continuity of operations plans.

At a Cloud Computing seminar in 2011, three IT executives from large-sized businesses discussed the relative maturity of Cloud Computing for their business. The title of the session was 'Is the Cloud Mature Enough for IT?'. However, all three agreed that the question was backwards. It's not 'is the Cloud mature enough for IT', but 'is IT mature enough for the Cloud'. Obviously, this question could be asked of any disruptive technology, since they all place demands on the business for which the business may not be prepared. The Web and e-commerce caught many businesses off guard in the mid-90s. Social media caught them off guard in the mid-2000s. Now, Cloud Computing and mobile devices have emerged as the next trend requiring the business's attention.

Unfortunately, in each of these cases, the business was forced to address change rapidly and then incorporate it into the processes of the business in a methodical fashion after the fact. This has downside risk for IT since the business identifies rapid response as success. However, this rapid response does not incorporate the needed controls and processes to limit negative impact to the business. To accomplish this, IT must implement repeatable and seemingly bureaucratic processes, which, in turn, have the net effect of sometimes frustrating the end-user, which is then negatively, albeit unfairly, reflected on IT.

This is analogous to a bunch of late people catching a bus that is driven recklessly and irresponsibly down the road at speeds well beyond the speed limit, but the people are making it to their destination on time. Then a new bus driver is hired who is more mature and has years of experience watching the wrecks of those less mature drivers, so they drive within the speed limit and obey all traffic laws. Needless to say, the passengers are not going to be very happy with this new bus driver; but the driver is needed and lowers the potential for risk of a fatal accident. Still, the net effect is that the driver is branded as a stalwart that can't deliver in 'business time', when the truth is the method used to get there fast was not sustainable.

Cheaper, faster, better! Pick any two! The motto continues to stand. Most likely Cloud Computing will follow a similar trend of rapid adoption, but eventually, the business will need to implement proper controls to ensure that the decision to use Cloud Computing is appropriate for the task and that it is adopted in a manner that ensures limited risk to the organisation.

Delivering IT-as-a-Service

It has been stated many times in many ways that to be successful in IT requires a triumvirate: people, process and technology. As illustrated in this chapter, the people component of that equation can be complex to work out and can raise the overall risk of a Cloud Computing initiative.

In many organisations, IT has become the target of criticism by the business. They are blamed for everything from why the desktop computer won't run properly to the reason the business didn't make their quota in the last quarter. Anecdotal evidence points to lack of customer service by IT as the primary reason behind this belief. Unfortunately, the perception that IT is a hurdle to doing business often comes out of the executive office and permeates throughout the hierarchy.

The CEO needs to be the champion for consistent and methodical execution provided by a well-oiled IT organisation. While 'cowboy' and 'skunkwork' projects are important scouting efforts, they should not be held up as the model of excellence. The business needs and must reward low-risk behaviour with regard to IT execution.

Likewise, IT needs to realise that they have an audience and serve that audience as would any good business leader. This is a key component of delivering IT-as-a-Service (ITaaS). Instead of being perceived as slum landlords forcing their tenants to make do, they need to be viewed as concierges servicing the tenants' needs and making them more productive. This is especially true with the options available to the business these days to circumvent the internal IT organisation. Being viewed in a negative way raises the overall risk of the business as a whole.

Additional resources

www.devops.com

www.cioinsight.com/c/a/Case-Studies/GM-Outsourcing-Overhaul-1-Year-Later/

www.cio.gov/documents/State-of-the-Federal-Datacentre-Consolidation-Initiative-Report.pdf

CHAPTER 8: BUSINESS CONTINUITY AND DISASTER RECOVERY IN CLOUD COMPUTING

Business continuity overview

A commonly used, but often misunderstood, phrase mentioned by corporate executives right down to the engineers in the networks team is 'business continuity'.

The best description I have heard used to reference business continuity would be to 'plan for things that you can expect to go wrong, but hope that they don't'. Whether we like to admit it or not, systems will fail, people will fail, natural disasters may well happen (depending on your geographical location this might become a more common occurrence than other locations), and, believe it or not, even the hallowed IT professionals make mistakes.

For the more theory-based readers, business continuity is best defined as: 'The development and exercising of a structured, methodological business plan to help minimise and reduce the risk of disruptions impacting the business.'

A business continuity plan (BCP) should provide a structured and documented process to ensure continuity and availability of business operations, in the event of unexpected circumstances.

While a common misconception is that business continuity is focused on platforms, technologies and buildings, it is people who hold the key to a successful business continuity programme. All the technologies, platforms and systems in the world could be available in the event of an interruption to business, but if the person who holds the passwords is unavailable, the business will not be able to continue.

The concept and principle I always encourage companies to use to form the foundation for their business continuity programme is that the scope includes people, processes and technology. (I refer to it as the PPT principle.) There is a valid reason why these are arranged in this order, which will be explained.

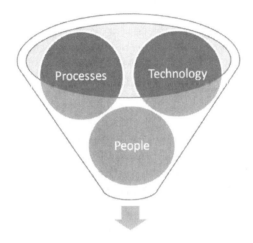

Figure 9: Foundations for an effective business continuity function

People – the essential element

While often referred to as the weakest link in the security chain, people can be the cause of a business continuity plan being invoked; but for those who have experienced a major business continuity incident at first hand, a cool, calm and collected individual who understands the business, its drivers and requirements, can be the most effective force in ensuring the timely resumption of business services.

When developing and documenting the business continuity plan and relevant team members, a cross-functional team made up from all the key departments from throughout the business should be chosen. When selecting the key members of the team, these members should possess a thorough and comprehensive understanding of their functions and the overall business – that's right, the overall business and the intricacies associated with the various functions, such as dependencies, restrictions and culture.

Processes

Business continuity processes form the core of the business continuity plan and serve to function as the reference points and associated activities or tasks for a specific section, function or area of the business. Processes, for those familiar with information security best-practice standards such as ISO27001, are often referred to as the 'work instructions, or how to', as they will provide the reader with detailed information on how the process is to be performed or operated from the users' perspective.

From a high level, processes provide the business continuity team members with the levels and type of information required to ensure the timely resumption of business operations.

Process flow charts provide a great visual overview of processes, their dependencies on other processes to fulfil their specified goal or objective. These can prove to be invaluable in a situation where parties are under pressure to restore, or ensure resumption of, critical business activities.

Technology

The reliance of organisations on technology and systems at all levels is never to be underestimated. A forward-thinking and proactive organisation will have a complete and comprehensive understanding of the systems and technologies in place both within their premises and externally. Knowing your dependencies when it comes to technology is an absolute must when creating or maintaining a business continuity plan. This can only be achieved by involving the correct personnel, teams and local knowledge in the area of key systems and technology.

While often taken for granted, technology failures, issues or lack of availability can (and do) often impact an overall business or specified business units significantly.

Depending on the business type, drivers and dependencies, the sudden loss of a key individual or key technological asset could have damning results on a business for the short, medium or long term.

A 'one size fits all' approach should never apply in business continuity planning. Organisations creating their business continuity plans using templates, or online resources, without investing the relevant time and effort on these plans, often tell these tales from new employment or professions!

A comprehensive and complete understanding is required by all parties involved in order to document, assess, analyse and report on the technologies currently used and/or required in the event of a disruption of business services.

Disaster recovery overview

Disaster recovery is your plan for the things you can't anticipate. These are things that are not accounted for or covered within the business continuity plan.

Disaster recovery planning is of particular importance in order to ensure that business operations can be maintained in the event of an unforeseen disaster or large-scale incident. A good approach to convey the meaning of disaster recovery would be to reference 'planes are falling from the sky' or 'a number of trucks crashed through our building'.

The selection of disaster recovery team members and structures are of particular importance when establishing or managing a disaster recovery function or capability. For organisations or professionals who are not fully familiar or do not hold any particular experience with disaster recovery, I would advise engaging an experienced (and credible) resource or entity to assist with this, as disaster recovery and business continuity can be vastly different in their goals and requirements.

A good and experienced independent resource could communicate and co-ordinate with the relevant stakeholders and senior executives throughout the organisation the importance and necessity for a disaster recovery function, with an emphasis on the team structures, make up and resourcing requirements.

BUSINESS   **DISASTER**
CONTINUITY **RECOVERY**

To help understand the difference between business continuity (BC) and disaster recovery (DR):

- BC is an on-going activity performed to ensure that critical business functions are available for those who require access.
- BC is not something implemented at the time of a disaster; business continuity refers to those activities performed daily to maintain service, consistency and recoverability.
- DR is the process, policies and procedures related to preparing for recovery or continuation of technology infrastructure critical to an organisation after a natural or human-induced disaster.

Adequate planning and support can ensure your business is on the right road to recovery in the event of business disruptions.

Differences between Cloud vs. traditional BC and DR

Like the introduction of any new technologies or platforms, Cloud Computing brings with it new risks. The goal of this chapter is to highlight some of the less acknowledged or addressed continuity risks and challenges.

A number of these risks and challenges can (or should) be addressed by the provider (depending on your agreement), and some by your organisation.

A few questions I like to pose to the organisations I meet with are as follows:

What happens in the event that the service is interrupted for an extended period of time?

What would happen if the provider gets into financial problems, or gets acquired by a larger entity with different continuity or service level agreements?'

If your organisation or a key service provider is unable to meet their financial obligations, how long will they continue to provide a service to you?

In an investigation of a crime, replacement of systems or migration to updated platforms, will your data remain available and protected in accordance with the service level agreement?'

Should you choose to switch Cloud providers or terminate the contract with your existing provider, can you obtain all your information in an intelligent and usable format?

Upon posing these questions and scenarios, you should be assured or get a sense of comfort that the Cloud provider has applied sufficient thought, introduced measures and provided measurable assurance of these results.

Always take the time to do your due diligence from a business continuity and disaster recovery point of view!

SaaS business continuity challenges

So your data is hosted in the Cloud. It gets regular scheduled and automated back-ups taken, stored and replicated across a number of geographic locations. Sounds foolproof? Not so fast!

First step for anyone availing themselves of SaaS offerings from a BC/DR point of view is to ensure an escrow agreement exists and operates as a functioning process for their data and applications. Ultimately, this agreement needs to be defined as part of the overall contract with the Cloud provider and details of the relevant escrow clause should at a minimum include obtaining regular dumps or slices of your organisation's data from multi-tenant deployments.

Additionally, while most SaaS vendors provide the ability for user acceptance testing (UAT) and quality assurance reviews online, customers should review the requirement for a similar solution re-created and available on-premises (or alternatively with another Cloud provider). This on-premises solution (or alternate Cloud provider) should be coupled with the data and application received under the relevant escrow agreement. This may not always be possible, but should be reviewed as an option from a continuity and recovery perspective.

Using the above will without doubt reduce the cost-benefit value proposition for an organisation, but could ultimately go a long way to mitigate, or reduce, the risk in terms of business continuity.

PaaS business continuity challenges

Just because the licensing aspect and provisioning of your platform has become almost instantaneous does not mean you can neglect the fundamentals! Your platform controls your environment, and everything that resides on it. In the event that your platform goes, so does most of your other related areas.

Microsoft has experienced outages to their Windows® Azure platform; if your organisation utilises this platform, your business could come to a grinding halt.

As a first step, ensure that the provider has a robust and assured Platform-as-a-Service (PaaS) solution for its enterprise customers.

Secondly, should the business keep a minimal number of platforms and licences available for business-critical servers? Why not? The investment may already have been made and could maximise the investment as a business continuity option.

Finally, review the organisation's requirements and platform interoperability. Repeatedly, organisations have the ability to migrate or move to a far more cost-effective or even free platform for their operations, but instead tend to stick with what they know. Change brings about opportunity – review the new opportunities to simplify and innovate.

IaaS business continuity challenges

The racks of equipment that made the communications room look like the inside of a NASA spaceship have now been elevated into the Cloud. So have the problems and challenges gone with it? That depends on the Cloud provider – same challenges, different playing field!

Hardware issues, performance issues, equipment failure and communication failure are all still very real risks that face businesses worldwide. Whether on or off premises, these are occurrences that will continue to disrupt business activities. So what can be done?

First, understand the environmental structure and interdependencies associated with the equipment. Get as much information as possible related to the environments, structures and locations of the data centres. Are the data centres or infrastructure farms built and maintained in line with best practice or certified to any standards? What measures are in place to facilitate failover, replication, interoperability and, ultimately, configuration changes?

Second, again look at the business critical assets and assess the likelihood of utilising initial investments in hardware to assist in the event of business disruptions to restore (even temporarily) critical, or core, infrastructure.

Possible benefits

The Cloud facilitates the service providers being able to offer on demand, off-site, flexible and scalable solutions, which from a business continuity point of view is of utmost importance to businesses and end-users alike.

By providing these hosted services, this assumes responsibility and takes the headache from the customer's hands. Depending on the service offerings, these tend to be offsite locations with resilience and adequate levels of physical security. With the data being held off-site, this can answer the question of 'what happens if our building goes up in flames' or 'how do we respond in the event of our primary facility becoming unavailable' – these all form an integral part of any effective business continuity plan and strategy.

Other benefits include the reduction in expenditure to purchase new hardware, software and equipment to facilitate business continuity. (Finance people just love this as it uses operational expenditure as opposed to capital expenditure and requires less spend from the outset.) This can facilitate more measurable and predictable spends related to business continuity, as most Cloud providers tend to promote these on a 'pay as you go' model. This is for now anyway, and might well change in the future!

Cloud Computing can facilitate and promote remote working or teleworking and allows organisations to reduce costs associated with traditional office-based computing. Businesses can then alter and adapt their work practices to utilise and manage their staff resources more effectively, enabling them to access data anytime anywhere – even if they are on the other side of the world. With the shift to more international links and business relationships being established on a daily basis, this is seen as a key growth area for Cloud Computing.

From a business continuity perspective, this is extremely beneficial. If for any reason personnel are unable to access the company's physical building or desk space, the company can continue to operate and provide services in line with their business requirements.

It is estimated that a total of around 20% of the American working population works from home or abroad at least once a month or more – further evidence that remote working is becoming a more common and required business process

Possible issues and challenges

While the above-mentioned benefits can vary depending on the organisation itself, the same will apply to the challenges or issues organisations might face. It should remain the priority of the organisation itself, and *not* the Cloud provider, to ensure adequate business continuity is in place.

There are a number of issues and challenges associated with selecting a Cloud business continuity solution. If an organisation already has working business continuity processes in place, it can be very challenging and complex to replicate to the Cloud – simply put, you will be removing the current controls or items within your environment and transferring them to the Cloud (however small or large this might be). The complete evaluation of technologies, platforms and or systems might need to be conducted in order to ensure that in the event of a business continuity incident, the information can be secured, accessed and maintained.

With an ever-increasing number of organisations becoming Cloud Computing providers, it is imperative to ensure that the service level agreement (SLA) and initial contract agreements pay special attention to business continuity, and that these are replicated with those currently in place within the environment.

It is very important for all parties concerned to have clearly defined SLAs before signing up to a Cloud service provider. I would encourage scheduled reviews and ongoing monitoring of compliance against these SLAs (*see Chapter 3* under *Governance*).

In essence, both parties should be completely clear on where their responsibilities do and do not end. A good and constant relationship should be established with those members of the Cloud service provider's team who will be involved in any business continuity exercises – after all, they will form an extension of your team in the event of business continuity simulations, exercises, walkthroughs and live scenarios.

Important considerations

Utilising the Cloud for key services, applications and/or platforms can seriously affect your business if they become unavailable.

As an example, if you locked all your information in a room that only had one key and that key became unavailable, what would that mean for your business.

In essence, if the Cloud provider's resources, platforms or environment became unavailable (for whatever reason), you will be unable to access all of your information. Liken it to being an online trading business and the Internet goes down.

By migrating to Cloud-based services or using Cloud service offerings, you are in essence becoming an online-based business, relying solely on your Cloud provider to remain online and secure. In anyone's books, that is a lot of trust to grant a single entity that can effectively control your business.

Whether you are internal to an organisation, acting as an advisor or consultant, the above-mentioned considerations should be used as an exercise to educate all parties involved. When these questions and scenario are used, it can serve as a great exercise to emphasise the reliance and dependency that an organisation will have with their Cloud provider – often the Cloud provider is an entity with which they do not have an existing or trusted relationship.

When reviewing or selecting service providers, it should be ensured that the SLA and relevant contracts are mapped and appropriate to the business. Never just select the most recognised, popular or biggest provider – as they more often than not are going to tailor their service offerings to your business needs, drivers or goals.

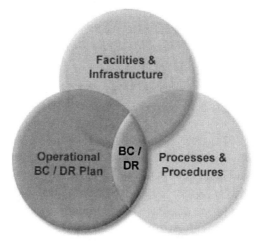

Figure 10: Elements of BC/DR

What to ask your Cloud provider

Asking questions makes your Cloud provider aware that you are serious about business continuity and the availability of your information. The first step is to understand the chain between the business you contract with and the one that provides the hosting facilities:

- Is the system hosted by one company or more?
- What is the financial health of each party in the chain?
- Is disaster recovery adequate for my requirements?
- Is data replicated over more than one site? How often?
- What are the back-up cycles (if back-up is included)?
- How often are recovery tests and business continuity exercises carried out?
- For multi-tenant systems, can recovery be made of just one tenant's system, if required?

- Do you hold any related certifications, or awards, recognising the business continuity processes in place within your environment (possibilities could include BS25999, ISO27001 or similar)?

Cloud-based BC and DR offerings

Businesses with limited budgets are discovering and utilising various aspects of Cloud Computing for business continuity and disaster recovery. With the need to purchase hardware and software being removed, data stored in the Cloud is on the servers of service providers. These providers tend to have various systems and servers at different locations that operate scheduled back-ups in accordance with the SLA and contract. This could be a minor part, a significant part or, in fact, all of the customer data that they receive.

Data saved in the Cloud should have a number of back-ups that can assist in data recovery for any material stored in it, depending on the retention periods defined for data back-up and the availability of this information.

This creates a redundancy that an individual business may find very expensive and complicated to duplicate. Do not assume that your provider will back up, retain and make this information available, as this will vary for each provider.

Other solutions and services offered could include backing up of all files, providing full system disk images of the systems, mail and web servers, and any other associated business systems.

The leading Cloud service providers offer a storage system, a file system and all applications necessary for a customer to have back-up and disaster recovery. It is worth noting that a number of the Cloud providers *do not* include the applications necessary, and will charge accordingly for these to be made available.

To ensure comprehensive data recovery, the Cloud provider will create replicas and secured images of all the protected systems, with the client deciding whether full, incremental or differential back-ups will be taken. These should be in line and governed by the business continuity or disaster recovery plans of the company utilising the Cloud service.

An untested back-up is the equivalent of no back-up at all. Ensure that back-ups are tested and reviewed regularly, whether it be on a back-up system, or in separate locations. Regular scheduled testing of back-ups is a valuable exercise and use of resources from a governance and training perspective.

Restructuring plans and procedures

As with any significant change to the business environment, a move to Cloud-based computing should trigger an immediate review and restructuring of related business continuity and disaster recovery plans. With the data locations, storage, mediums and data retention being altered, the plans will need to be reviewed in line with other processes. A number of plan changes might be triggered during this exercise including (but not limited to):

- scope
- business impact analysis/assessment
- recovery time objectives

- process and/or system dependencies
- asset inventory
- business owners
- emergency response teams
- change management.

As these items might now reside with a different entity, process owner or asset owner, the responsibilities will need to be restructured and documented accordingly. If new roles and personnel have become involved, further training and awareness should be provided prior to testing of plans according to the new structures.

Testing and walkthrough of updated plans

Both business continuity and disaster recovery plans are not worth the paper they are documented on until they have been communicated, understood and tested sufficiently. There are various types and methods of testing possible, which can range from simple to very complex and detailed. The key to successful business continuity and disaster recovery testing is to incorporate regular scheduled testing as part of the overall business continuity/disaster recovery management process.

All tests require the support of senior management, as well as time and availability of resources, possible costs and reporting mechanisms from engagement to completion. Teams and businesses who are familiar with and well versed in business continuity and disaster recovery testing tend to fair far better than those who do not, and by incorporating testing into scheduled and set review timelines, this could be the difference between saving or losing your business in the event of a disaster or business interruption.

Three fundamental test types are used in business continuity testing: the plan review, tabletop test and simulation tests. Let's examine each briefly:

- *Plan review/assessment* The BC/DR plan owner and team review and assess the existing the BC/DR plan. The team and owner review the document(s) in detail, looking for missing plan elements and inconsistencies with areas for improvement.
- *Tabletop test* In a tabletop test, the relevant participants and team members gather in a room to walk through plan activities step by step. Tabletop exercises can provide good insight as to the knowledge of the team members and knowing their roles in the event of an emergency or disruption. Tabletop exercises can also identify documentation errors, missing information, inaccurate details and inconsistencies.
- *Walkthrough test* In a walkthrough test, the team members and participants physically walk through the test within the environment (where possible) to assess the effectiveness of the business continuity or disaster recovery plan. Walkthrough tests cover the same aspects of the tabletop; however, they are typically conducted in a real-world environment.
- *Partial simulation* Partial simulation tests are performed on selected business units with full details and scope being reviewed. They are planned with the view to not risk any disruptions to normal business operations. These simulations are not as comprehensive as the full simulation but can serve a critical function in identifying areas for improvement or shortfalls.

- *Full simulation test* This is also known as a 'mock disaster test', its purpose being to simultaneously assess as many aspects or components of the business as possible. Full simulations are likely to be costly, could disrupt normal business operations and should only be conducted with caution. Adequate time for preparation must be given prior to conducting testing. Full tests do not require the primary site and systems to be halted, as they are conducted on the live environments.

To determine if procedures and resources work in a more realistic situation, a simulation test is desirable. It uses established business continuity resources, such as recovery sites, back-up systems and other specialised services.

In order for processes and management systems to improve in a measurable and proactive manner, use of the Deming life cycle should be utilised wherever possible.

For those familiar with ISO27001, BS25999 and other quality management systems/frameworks, the Deming life cycle is a continuous process conducted at both set intervals and on an ongoing basis. It looks to promote continual improvement and advancement of processes in a sustainable and measurable manner and focuses on the four key steps of Plan, Do, Check and Act.

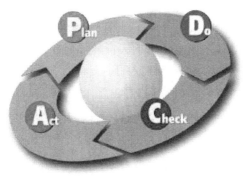

Figure 11: Deming life cycle for continual improvement.

Recent business continuity/disaster recovery case study

Amazon Web Services

On 21 April 2011, Amazon Web Services (otherwise known as AWS) Elastic Compute Cloud (EC2), based in Northern Virginia, went offline, affecting a number of their Cloud Computing customers, including Reddit, Foursquare, Quora, Paper.li and Mobypicture.

Amazon were quick to cite 'network latency' and 'connectivity errors' as the cause for the loss of service, and denied it was the subject of a malicious attack or hack. The outage caused both Amazon and its clients significant embarrassment, coupled with loss of earnings. Quora, one of the clients affected by the loss of service posted a 'down' message on their site, and responded with a quote stating: 'We'd point fingers, but we wouldn't be where we are today without EC2.' Quora also went on to release a YouTube video poking fun at the incident, along with Foursquare.com who posted a banner stating 'Sorry! We are having technical difficulties. Brief planned downtime tonight!'

While no figures have been released or details on costs incurred for Amazon or their clients housed in the Northern Virginia Data Centre, it is estimated that Amazon could have lost millions of dollars in prospective clients who were reviewing Amazon (EC2) as a Cloud provider.

Of key concern was the premise that Amazon had multiple availability zones to avoid any outages. The AWS region that went down was in Northern Virginia, leaving the remainder of their regions as two in the United States (one east coast, one west coast), one in Europe (Ireland) and two in Asia (Tokyo, Singapore). Each region has within it multiple 'Availability Zones' (AZs), which are supposed to be isolated, so that they have no single point of failure less than a natural disaster or something of that magnitude.

AWS stated that by 'launching instances in separate AZs, you can protect your applications and information from failure of a single location'. In reality, none of this really mattered as the point is that AZs should fail independently until a catastrophic failure occurs.

Essentially, AWS had misled or broken their promises to their clients on the failure scenarios for AZs. It meant that AWS had a common single point of failure.

Partial services were being restored by the second day of outages, with some clients taking an additional few days before being back online and fully operational.

The question then posed was: 'Could your business have survived this sort of outage from a Cloud provider?'

Additional resources

For those of who are interested in learning more about the various aspects of business continuity and disaster recovery, the following links can provide additional information:

Business Continuity Institute

http:\\www.thebci.org/

DRI International (previously known as Disaster Recovery Institute)

www.drii.org/

British Standards Institute (BSI), BS25999 – Business Continuity Standard

www.bsigroup.com

CHAPTER 9: INVESTIGATIONS AND FORENSICS IN THE CLOUD

Cloud Computing forensics is currently an unknown by both Cloud providers and Cloud customers due to its immaturity and lack of Cloud investigations conducted. This is an area that is set to develop extensively in the next few years. At present, no formal mechanisms, methodologies or standards have been developed for Cloud forensics.

The goal of this chapter is to promote thought and insight into the changes and challenges introduced in digital forensic investigations when in a Cloud environment.

As yet, there is no solution – no commercial forensic tools have been developed for Cloud Computing platforms, nor are there any certifications for this field.

Additionally, this chapter looks to provide some education at a high level to the average business reader who may have limited knowledge of digital forensics along with the challenges it presents for both traditional and Cloud environments.

Forensics overview

Computer forensic investigations use specialist and highly sophisticated tools to analyse information in a safe and non-corrupting fashion (i.e. they do not change any of the data or information at the source – thus leaving it intact for legal reasons).

E-discovery is the collection of evidence from a number of locations or sources including a network or networked systems. Both forensics and e-discovery will continue to form a necessary component of a proactive, forward-thinking and effective information security programme.

Investigations and forensics in Cloud Computing are somewhat of an unknown by most organisations. Few organisations have given adequate thought to what might happen or be required if a forensic investigation is initiated or required for legal reasons.

Why are forensic investigations initiated?

A forensic case or examination is triggered for any of the following reasons:

- criminal investigation
- civil case
- suspected illicit or illegal materials
- copyright or intellectual property disputes
- fraudulent activities
- disciplinary case
- security data breach
- regulatory request.

Usually, a forensic investigation is carried out at the request of senior management, board members, law enforcement bodies or at the request of a court of law when unusual events or circumstances are suspected, alerted or reported.

Current pressures and factors

In today's world of strict regulations, increasing cybercrime, insider threats, fraud and theft, technical and forensic investigations form an integral part of an organisation's overall information security framework (in larger organisations, this might form part of a separate function, such as compliance, audit, etc.).

As well as identifying direct evidence of a crime, digital forensics can be used to attribute evidence to specific suspects or events, confirm alibis or statements, and determine intent or cause.

Forensics: what has changed?

In two words – Cloud Computing!

By moving data, the traditional mechanisms, such as the platform on which it is housed, is now removed from the equation as a first step in the forensic process. So what? Surely we can just acquire, image and investigate as necessary?

Not necessarily so! Traditionally, the environments or devices being subjected to a technical examination would reside on site or in a known location, which could be obtained and investigated accordingly. With departments and devices now adopting Cloud Computing for certain elements, processes or functions, the traditional mechanisms and systems utilised are now no longer involved.

With Cloud Computing removing the traditional on-premises systems, the location, accessibility and ability to gather data may be altered significantly.

We will outline the key differences between traditional environments and Cloud environments and how these changes can affect all parties concerned later in this chapter.

Who conducts these investigations?

Traditionally, and wherever possible, an organisation will engage a qualified and experienced forensic investigator (either as an individual or as an entity).

There are a number of very valid reasons for doing this including legal, expertise, experience and advanced technical skills required to conduct forensic investigations.

Any organisation that has previously experienced the time-consuming and costly prosecution or criminal trial involving digital evidence will bear testament that a competent, certified and experienced digital investigator can make this process far less painful, and result in the desired outcome.

The often very sensitive nature of investigations requires ongoing communications and dealings with lawyers, solicitors, law enforcement, courts, senior business executives and stakeholders for lengthy periods of time.

This requires both a highly experienced and qualified professional with a thorough understanding of forensic practices.

Ultimately, this person or entity should be able to interpret findings and evidence in a clear and concise manner for presentation to the appropriate audiences.

Forensic procedures and requirements

When dealing with a forensic investigation, there are five stages that need to be followed to ensure the integrity of the digital evidence.

A suitably qualified and experienced professional investigator should carry out these stages.

Figure 12: Stages in a computer forensic investigation

1. Preparation and approach

This is the background information obtained to educate the investigator on any issues, complexities or obstacles they might encounter and establish the goals for the investigation. The following requirements would be typical of the preparation and approach stage:

- standards and policies being used by the organisation;
- policies and procedures implemented within the organisation which will affect the investigation;
- preventative and or detective controls in place;
- technical controls and methods for the collection of evidence and associated information;
- training of onsite resources/personnel concerned;
- legal advice;
- notification to the relevant authorities (if deemed or a possible criminal case);

- selection of forensic toolset (depending on the organisation or jurisdiction, there might be a preference).

2. Gathering data

In order to gather data effectively throughout the investigation, documentation is the key. Many times a forensic case goes wrong or encounters issues due to poor investigator's notes. These investigations can go on for weeks, months and even years, so correct, concise records are essential to any case. A documented and regimented structure from beginning to end is recommended, which is clear, concise and can be understood by other investigators, law enforcement officers or anyone else who might be involved in the investigation at a later stage. The following actions would be typical of the gathering data stage:

- obtaining a forensic image of the target device;
- transporting the evidence to a secure environment;
- verifying the integrity of the evidence;
- searching for and identifying evidence on a computer;
- storage of evidence.

3. Analysing results

The investigator now examines the evidence with extensive analysis carried out in accordance with the objectives and requirements. The analysis stage is often the most time-consuming stage, which includes significant interaction with the organisation in question, the entity or body acting on the organisation's behalf.

The following actions would be typical of the analysis stage:

- examining evidence using selected tools (finding the information or evidence agreed in the preparation stage);
- analysing (examination of findings to determine the significance and value of the evidence found);
- communicating and corresponding with the point of contact regarding findings, updates and other relevant information.

4. Compiling report

A comprehensive investigation can be undone by sub-standard or poor reporting. In the event of a criminal investigation, a successful prosecution can often rely entirely on a forensic investigator's report.

The following information is typical of the reporting levels required:

- executive summary
- case timeline and objectives
- evidence and criteria analysed
- relevant findings (state fact vs. opinion)
- supporting evidence
- relevant additional information and recommendations.

5. Present findings

Besides presenting facts, forensic reports and presentations provide an opportunity for the investigator to communicate their expert opinion to those within the organisation. It also provides those parties concerned with an opportunity to understand and query the findings from the investigator. One point worth noting is that documented reports can be misread, misinterpreted or misconstrued: presenting the findings of the report can greatly assist in reducing opportunities for this to occur.

Forensic investigations vs. analysis

Investigations are much broader in scope than other areas of forensic analysis. The usual aim of forensic analysis is to provide answers to a series of questions; a full investigation often involves large amounts of information and complex timelines, and can rely on numerous other devices or items in order to verify the integrity of the information.

Aside from identifying evidence for the investigation of crime, forensic examinations and techniques are used to attribute evidence to specific suspects, confirm alibis or statements, determine intent or efforts, identify sources and authenticate documents.

Traditional forensics vs. Cloud forensics

Traditionally, an organisation or entity would identify a machine or device, which is then seized (in accordance with the key steps and stages 'Forensic procedures and requirements', outlined earlier in this chapter) and sent to a forensic lab for analysis.

During the preparation stage, the investigator would have obtained an understanding, history, background and overview of the environment, possible actions and what is required from the organisation or entity in order to commence the investigation. This, however, is now changing and becoming far more challenging for organisations and investigators alike. Two examples of this might be:

- How do you know if the user has been utilising Cloud services (either from the organisation itself, or from the user's personal standpoint)?
- If they have, where was the information sent, stored or transmitted?
- Is the information still available?
- Who owns the information?
- What fragments or traces remain of the information?
- Can these areas be investigated or assessed as part of the analysis?

These are just some of the questions that will need to be assessed prior to commencing the investigation, and are referred to as 'scoping'.

Techniques and information that an investigator might use to ascertain if the user has used Cloud-based services could include:

- Internet analysis and Internet history
- browser activity
- cookies
- temporary files and Internet files
- favourites and bookmarked sites
- automated tasks or scripts
- last accessed and login details
- use of unusual proxies
- creation of new accounts and e-mail addresses
- use of IP and address-masking software.

The above steps and actions could provide valuable information and details as to the user's behaviour relevant to the investigation scope. More often than not, investigators find that instances of wrongdoing or breaches of policy tend to be repeated numerous times, and what might start as a simple forensic analysis, unearths things that will change the scope of the initial investigation.

In identifying that the user has been using Cloud services, the following steps should be taken by the organisation, entity and forensic investigator:

- contact the Cloud service provider;
- explain the situation;
- request the relevant information required;
- request the format and level of information required;
- request the user's files (in an intelligent and structured format);
- request the user's access logs.

However, involving a Cloud service provider in a forensic investigation can become frustrating for those involved with budget, time constraints and reliance on a third party with whom you have no relationship. Typically, the following problems are presented:

- no forensic procedure or process in place
- international laws and jurisdictions
- time delays
- cost of obtaining the information (most providers will not give you the information and details for free – if at all!)
- nature of the organisation itself (most Cloud providers are focusing on gaining customers, not losing them)
- size, type and bureaucracy of the Cloud provider.

Encountering a responsive and hassle-free forensic investigation involving a Cloud provider is rare; preparation and understanding of limitations is imperative.

Why is this? Surely they are obliged to do so? Well, that depends on the fine print! Cloud providers are concerned with the privacy of their clients (in multi-tenant environments), the costs associated with obtaining, retrieving and providing the information, and any possible reputational or qualitative damage they might incur.

As much of a shock as this might be, Cloud service providers are more interested in selling 'one size fits all' service offerings to organisations than responding to information requests, legal correspondence and assisting forensic investigators who are not paying customers.

Ultimately, providers are required to respond to law enforcement/state entities, whereas they may not be required to do so for commercial clients.

Data in transit

With investigations involving a structured environment, such as a LAN, WAN or VLAN, there would be sources and means by which information is transmitted from the device in question to other various network points or platforms. Examples of these could include switches, routers, firewalls, intrusion detection systems (IDS), intrusion prevention systems (IPS) and other forms of technical controls that are capturing traffic information.

This is not the same for Cloud investigations. Depending on the structure of the target environment, the same level of control, monitoring, reporting and information might not exist. For example, what types of information are required, and is this information available from the Cloud provider?

- In what format is it available?

- Is this source of information true and accurate?
- Is it from the original source?
- Can the integrity of this information be trusted?

Encryption and investigations

Organisations serious about Cloud Computing security ensure that their information is encrypted using a suitable level of encryption (a minimum of the NIST/US Department of Defence standard of encryption would be a good guideline for those who are not specialist in this area).

Another item that has recently made headlines regarding encryption and Cloud Computing is the capability for some Cloud providers to decrypt information if required.

This is relevant to the US Patriot Act (which allows the US Government to review information in the interests of national security) requiring the decryption of information when necessary for review or investigation. This includes Cloud providers having the capability to decrypt information if requested to do so under the US Patriot Act.

This does, however, raise the question that if the Cloud provider has the capability to decrypt information, who is responsible for ensuring the relevant information is not being viewed or decrypted for other reasons?

Custom Cloud APIs

The world of Cloud Computing is currently built using application programming interfaces (APIs). Cloud APIs utilise a set of commands to interact with Cloud services to request data and actions.

The current issues concerning Cloud APIs and those conducting investigations are that the vast majority of Cloud providers create vendor-specific APIs. To conduct a forensic investigation involving a Cloud platform, an investigator would need to capture and interpret the commands of the API, identify the user's actions and data accessed, and identify the time and date of access – no small task taking into account the vast amount of time and resources used to create an API by the Cloud provider.

Cloud solution forensic tools

In terms of technology, Cloud-based computing is a fairly new and rapidly evolving landscape with few regulations, a lack of legislation and, most importantly for forensic investigators, few Cloud forensic tools.

With only a handful of established (and credible) digital forensic toolkits available around the world today, the reality is that these tools were never developed with the Cloud in mind, and as such are not fit for purpose. These existing tools were designed with real-time systems in mind and not for virtualised environments that are shared, scattered and may be required for hundreds of different uses simultaneously.

In summary

Unfortunately for the forensic investigators and those organisations who find themselves starting a forensic investigation, the individuals being investigated or actions being examined might well stand a good chance of their actions escaping or being undetected. The additional steps and barriers introduced by Cloud Computing could, in fact, hide or mask these actions in places and environments that the investigator and the parties concerned may be unable to access, interpret or legally enter. Taking into account the immaturity of the Cloud Computing market, it has become apparent that most Cloud providers have little to no formalised and implemented forensic or digital investigation plans, policies or procedures.

As yet, there are no structured or formalised Cloud security standards that highlight or outline the recommended stages, steps or processes that should be in place to conduct, facilitate or assist with forensic investigations. Until these are introduced, I envisage an uphill battle for all those who find themselves conducting forensic investigations where the Cloud has been involved.

If these challenges do not seem daunting enough, we will also discuss the international implications of Cloud Computing in *Chapter 10*.

Additional resources

For those of who are interested in learning more about the various aspects of digital forensic investigations, the following links can provide additional information:

SANS Computer Forensics Blog

http://computer-forensics.sans.org

Access Data Corporation

www.accessdata.com

Guidance Software

www.guidancesoftware.com

US-CERT Computer Emergency Readiness Team

http://www.us-cert.gov/

CHAPTER 10: CLOUD COMPUTING BORDERS – NATIONAL AND INTERNATIONAL DEPLOYMENT

Notwithstanding the benefits gained from Cloud Computing, Cloud Computing can introduce a number of legal and international challenges for your organisation.

From an international legal perspective, the key difference between traditional IT outsourcing and Cloud Computing is *where* the data resides, is processed and stored. Data can (and almost always is) be stored in various locations, data centres and different jurisdictions all over the world and across multiple platforms. This can result in multiple copies of data being stored and processed in different locations.

The Cloud revolutionises the term 'outsourcing' and introduces numerous implications of outsourced data handling, contract terms and conditions, intellectual property rights and insurance coverage. These are some of the most encountered issues for those new to outsourcing and Cloud Computing. There are numerous other elements that should be assessed and addressed with the help of qualified and experienced Cloud Computing legal experts.

We are by no means claiming to be legal experts; the primary objective of this chapter is to illustrate and communicate *some* of the many legal aspects associated with Cloud Computing.

As with all elements of Cloud Computing, if in any doubt regarding organisational requirements, obligations and legal rights, contact a legal professional who specialises in Cloud Computing (or outsourcing agreements) to assist in the due diligence review of Cloud provider contracts and agreements.

Regardless of organisation type, business objectives, drivers, business sectors or mission, the following points should be assessed and understood.

Data location

Depending on where data is at any given time will dictate which laws and legislation govern it. This will also include the terms and conditions of the contract, and will impact on any disputes, settlements and privacy laws affecting the locations and jurisdictions involved.

Assumption is the worst possible mistake when determining data location.

Keep in mind is that even though data may be housed within your legal jurisdiction, the contract and service level agreement (SLA) might be from an international parent company located in a different geographical location, thereby falling under different laws.

In all contracts, SLAs and associated agreements including data protection and privacy, it is imperative to ensure the exact location and jurisdictions involved, as this can prevent or hinder the application and enforcement of the contractual terms.

Legislation and regulatory (including privacy)

Each jurisdiction provides stringent rules on defence, health, and financial services related information, which directly impact on Cloud Computing. Stringent regulatory provisions and restrictions concerning the transfer of certain types of data across borders and export or trade restrictions may impact on where data in the Cloud can be stored and who can store it or on the transfer itself of the data and applications to and from the Cloud.

Data protection and data privacy

Data protection and privacy is, without doubt, one of the largest headaches for multinational corporations based across several countries, continents and different jurisdictions. Data protection and privacy regulations often vary greatly depending on the country in question, irrelevant of partner relationships. An example of this would be that certain EU Members States' data protection laws contradict the EU data privacy acts. France and Germany are renowned for legislation that does not comply with other European data protection rules.

In contrast to the United States (discussed later in this chapter), in Europe privacy is a human right.

Data retention

An often overlooked and less considered aspect of Cloud Computing is how long the data is held for. Why does it matter? There are various legal and regulatory reasons, depending on the nature of the organisation, industry and jurisdictions that require organisations to retain data for specific periods of time.

Unfortunately, most organisation do not specify this in Cloud contracts, SLAs and contract negotiations, resulting in legal and regulatory requirements not being fulfilled prior to migration.

Data types should be listed, understood and defined in accordance with relevant retention periods.

Retaining information indefinitely, for unspecified time periods is not good practice, and eventually can come back to haunt organisations.

EU Data Protection/Privacy

Under recently revised and updated EU data protection acts, the following provide key aspects for companies to consider:

These directives were required to be implemented into local laws on 25 May 2011. The following European States are all required to comply with the EU Data Protection and Privacy Directive as per requirements outlined for all 27 Member States: Austria, Belgium, Bulgaria, Cyprus, Czech Republic, Denmark, Estonia, Finland, France, Germany, Greece, Hungary, Ireland, Italy, Latvia, Lithuania, Luxembourg, Malta, Netherlands, Poland, Portugal, Romania, Slovakia, Slovenia, Spain, Sweden and the United Kingdom.

Additionally, Andorra, Argentina, Faroe Islands, Guernsey, Isle of Man, Israel, Jersey and Switzerland have been approved as their data protection and privacy principles satisfy those of the EU. Canada has received approval for certain types of personal data, but as yet has not obtained full acceptance from the EU.

EU Data Protection Directive 95/46/EC

The EU Data Protection Directive 95/46/EC outlines the requirements and guidelines for all organisations collecting personal information from data subjects.

The EU Directive on Data Protection of 1995 mandated that each EU nation create and pass a national privacy law for a Data Protection Authority. The function of this Data Protection Authority is to protect citizens' privacy and investigate breaches or failures to do so.

The EU Data Protection Directive focuses on personal information, which is categorised as 'any information relating to an identified or identifiable natural person', known as the 'data subject'. A data subject is a living and identifiable person who can be identified (directly or indirectly) by reference to one or more factors specific to their physical, physiological, mental, economic, cultural or social identity.

While this might be somewhat vague and subjective, the spirit of the EU Data Protection Directive looks to encompass any significant pieces of information that could link that information to a living identifiable individual.

The 'data controller' refers to a legal person, public authority, agency or any other body which alone or jointly with others determines the purposes and means of the processing of personal data; where the purposes and means of processing are determined by national or Community laws or regulations. The data controller is typically the person who collects the information from the data subject.

A 'data processor' refers to a natural or legal person, public authority, agency or any other body that processes personal data on behalf of the controller. In today's world many organisations will utilise outside agencies or contractors to conduct activities on their behalf – for instance, marketing, support and related activities.

These agencies and third parties are data processors, as they are processing information on data subjects on behalf of the data controller.

It is important to note that while the data processor may be in possession of the information, it remains the ultimate responsibility of the data controller to adhere to the key principles and guidelines of the EU Data Protection Directive throughout the life cycle of the information or data.

EU Data Protection Requirements

Under the EU Data Protection Directive 95/46/EC, all data controllers collecting personal information are required to ensure the following guidelines and principles are adhered to at all times (slight variations may occur depending on local laws and regulations):

- Obtain and process the information fairly.
- Keep it only for one or more specified and lawful purposes.
- Process it only in ways compatible with the purposes for which it was given initially.
- Keep it safe and secure.
- Keep it accurate and up to date.
- Ensure that it is adequate, relevant and not excessive.
- Retain it no longer than is necessary for the specified purpose or purposes.

- Data subjects should be allowed to access their data and make corrections to any inaccurate data.

An important article in the Directive is: 'It shall remain the responsibility of the data controller to ensure that the above mentioned items are complied with.'

For those who fail to adhere to these clauses, these failures can be met with significant financial penalties, imprisonment (which is rare in the majority of cases, with only a handful of convictions leading to imprisonment) and the prevention of future data collection and processing. Depending on the countries themselves, the enforcement tends to be wide and varied.

For instance, in the United Kingdom the fines imposed by the Information Commissioner's Office can be up to £500,000, subject to the findings of an investigation (this number was increased in 2010 following a large number of high-profile data breaches and losses of personal information). For most organisations, this is a significant penalty to pay for non-compliance or a data breach that could have been prevented.

Separately, while instances of imprisonment are rare, recent cases in the United Kingdom have shown that those in 'positions of power' who knowingly breach the Data Protection Act will face significant actions.

In April 2011, Karen Howie, a 34-year-old police constable from Scotland, breached the Data Protection Act when she took details of an investigation from police computers and passed them onto her partner, who used the details to warn a suspect. Howie subsequently received a 27-month sentence for the disclosure of these details.

Duty to report breaches

In recent amendments to EC requirements, the Directive 2009/136/EC of The European Parliament and of The Council of 25 November 2009 includes:

amending Directive 2002/22/EC on universal service and users' rights relating to electronic communications networks and services, Directive 2002/58/EC concerning the processing of personal data and the protection of privacy in the electronic communications sector and Regulation (EC) No 2006/2004 on co-operation between national authorities responsible for the enforcement of consumer protection laws.

Article 2 (2) (4) (c) adds a requirement to notify security breaches to 'national authority' and to those affected by this vulnerability, at least if the flaw is 'likely to affect negatively' their personal data.

While these changes require notification of security breaches to the relevant national authority, many organisations continue not to do so. Most breaches are currently reported 'voluntarily' by organisations that communicate and co-ordinate with the relevant authorities, before contacting the individuals concerned.

Recent reporting trends

Depending on the size, structure and nature of organisations who find themselves in the unenviable position of having suffered a data protection breach, a somewhat worrying trend has begun to emerge.

Recently, a number of organisations have informed customers of data breaches or data loss by letter, email or press releases. These materials often highlight very standard methods of protection applied to the devices or data affected, such as passwords, in an attempt to reassure those affected of the data's security.

Any information security practitioner worth their professional credentials would seriously challenge these statements. Password protection can often by bypassed or cracked by either an experienced IT savvy person or by a number of freeware and low-cost applications within minutes.

Password protection and other standard methods of security are no longer effective against current threats and targeted cyberattacks. Cybercriminals and malicious hackers are becoming highly successful at compromising and exploiting traditional methods of security to obtain commercially valuable and sensitive information.

Recent events have been examples of why organisations should be proactive and be forthcoming in the event of data breaches. Sony, Citigroup and a number of other headline grabbers in 2011 have left a lot to be desired, especially the manner and means by which they decided to postpone, deny and refute claims that their relevant standards, processes and procedures ultimately led them to fail and in return leave 100 million+ individuals to possibly pay for their mistakes.

Should your organisation fall victim to any of these attacks, or, indeed, experience data breaches, leaks of information, data corruption or similar issues, it is often discovered that openness, honesty and transparency can go a long way when dealing with those who have been affected!

European Privacy Directive 2002/58/EC

Confidentiality requirements

The European Privacy Directive 2002/58/EC was designed, and introduced to address the emergence of mobile devices and the processing of personal data in the electronic communications sector. While not as widely known and acknowledged as the European Data Protection Act, the Privacy Directive plays an important role outlining the requirements for privacy, security and the governance of services for publicly available electronic communications.

Aside from defining the security requirements (without explicitly stating levels of security) the Privacy Directive focuses on the important aspect of confidentiality.

For those familiar with information security and the three core pillars on which it is founded (confidentiality, integrity and availability), this should be commonplace. However, never underestimating the requirements to ensure confidentiality will go a long way to staying compliant with the Privacy and Data Protection Directives.

The Confidentiality of Communications section in the Directive places emphasis on the European Member States to ensure that the following aspects of communications and related traffic data over public communications and publicly available systems are adhered to.

The following actions are prohibited, and are required to be enforced through national legislation:

- listening, tapping, storage or other kinds of interception or surveillance of communications;

- and the related traffic data by persons other than users of the relevant services, without the explicit consent of these users concerned.

These actions are not permitted, except in the case where the organisation is legally authorised to do so, and then this must be in accordance with relevant laws and directives of that jurisdiction or country.

Measuring compliance against these prohibited actions might prove a challenge for any organisation.

Current EU data protection and privacy challenges

Technology

With technology evolving and being replaced at such a rapid rate, it is understandable that the law and policy makers are going to be playing 'catch up'. As changes in national laws and legislations can take years to complete, and then additional time to transfer into practice, regulations and laws will, for the foreseeable future, be lagging behind.

With current financial pressures being felt throughout the EU and worldwide, efforts are understandably focused on economic recoveries and ensuring long-term viability. These times should be when the EU states are boosting their efforts to ensure legislation and relevant laws are brought up to speed and in line with other technology-leading nations (Ireland, Malta, Denmark, Sweden, Switzerland, and the United Kingdom), which have ensured such laws exist in an effort to protect citizens and personnel.

Many of these nations (particularly Ireland) are promoting themselves as excellent places to do business and provide technology-related services. Ireland alone has had significant investment (in the billions of euros/dollars) from companies, such as Dell, Microsoft, Google, Salesforce, EMC, Oracle and a number of other Cloud Computing providers. Many other EU nations are attracting significant investments along with Ireland.

In order for these investments (and further investment) from other multinationals to continue, many of these nations' governments have placed particular emphasis on ensuring relevant laws and legislations are met.

Never more so than at present has the focus been on data protection, and data privacy between organisations and citizens alike. Until such time that a uniform approach is taken by all nations and parties involved to implement practices according to the required regulations and requirements, the Internet and Cloud Computing will continue to pose numerous challenges and headaches.

Cookies

Recent developments and changes to the EU Privacy and Electronic Communications Directive now require the 27 Member States to pass into law rules regarding websites, and specifically the log data collected about the visitors to the sites.

This law has caused a fair amount of debate and criticism from certain circles; however, it is not all bad. The law came into effect on 26 May 2011, and requires website owners to obtain consent from site visitors to put a cookie on their computer. For those website owners out there, approximately 90% of websites in use today currently utilise cookies to log traffic to their websites. These include Google Analytics™, WordPress Blogs and WordPress plugins along with other website development tools and platforms.

There are a number of different cookies currently used by developers, including session, persistent, secure, third-party cookies and others depending on the requirements of the relevant website.

Cookies are short text files placed in the user's computer and used to collect and communicate information between the target website and the device accessing that website. Cookies play an important function for those websites requiring login for user activity (authentication), for the identification of a user and for e-commerce-related sites, such as shopping carts, booking of flights, tickets and anything similar, to track the state of a transaction.

Cookies can also collect information about users, such as geographical location, pages accessed, time spent on each page and functions performed (depending on which type of cookie is being used).

This level of information can provide invaluable information for those website owners to ensure the website performs and functions in accordance with the user requirements and focuses on user demands.

However, cookies are commonly targeted by spyware attacks and in attempts to track user activities online. These include cross-site scripting attacks, session hijacks, to complete theft of cookies.

It is now illegal for websites to collect this information, under various EU and US privacy and data protection laws, without obtaining consent from its users. The viewpoint from the EU on this is that the majority of website users are unaware of this, and as such are not giving their consent for this information to be collected, thus breaching the Directive.

The use of cookies on a website without the user's consent constitutes the access and collection of personal information without the consent of the user – a violation of the Data Protection Directive and the site user's privacy.

However, cookies are not being banned or required to be removed from websites. The EU Directive requires the website owner to inform and notify users of the cookies being used and ask for their permission to collect the relevant information. For experienced organisations, a simple pop-up or checkbox informing users of this requirement will suffice and allow the use of cookies to continue; for those who do not incorporate this or suitable other mechanisms, some issues may be encountered further down the line.

At present, The United Kingdom Information Commissioner's Office (Data Protection Office) has granted a 12-month period (as of 26 May 2011) for UK organisations to comply with the Directive; however, this is not applicable to all EU nations.

A good reference for those looking to publish a statement or pop-up to notify their users of this change and ensure permission can be found at the Information Commissioner's Office website (*www.ico.gov.uk*).

Where to next for EU data protection?

On 25 January 2012, the European Commission proposed a comprehensive reform of the EU's 1995 data protection rules. These proposed changes strengthen online privacy rights and boost Europe's digital economy. The Commission has now published its draft proposals to replace the general Data Protection Directive 95/46/EC with a more detailed Regulation that would apply directly throughout the EU.

The changes put forward in the document are done so with the intention of having EU data protection law apply in a uniform way across the Member States (with a single set of rules for all to play by).

Most notable of these proposed changes is the general requirement to report serious data breaches as soon as possible to the national supervisory authority (if possible within 24 hours).

Other changes include the requirement on companies employing over 250 people (and certain other organisations) to appoint a data protection officer.

Notably for multinational organisations, they will only have to deal with a single national data protection authority in the EU country where they have their main establishment (a one-stop shop).

At present these are only at a draft proposal stage, and are yet to be confirmed or signed into law. The draft proposed changes can be found at the following link: *http://ec.europa.eu/justice/newsroom/data-protection/news/120125_en.htm*

United States data protection and privacy

The United States (in contrast to the EU) seems to take a more 'relaxed' approach to data protection and privacy, particularly regarding universal legislation for data protection across the United States.

At present, there is no comprehensive data protection legislation across the United States, merely a segregated patchwork combination of legislation, regulatory requirements and self-regulation to govern concepts of data protection.

Interestingly, the word 'privacy' does not appear anywhere in the US Constitution, while it is referenced in parts within the Bill of Rights, such as the Fourth Amendment.

While this might come as a bit of a surprise to some, there are quite a number of valid reasons why a single framework does not exist. This may be a culture thing more than anything else.

Let's face it, Americans have become accustomed to be subjected to a prying government that insists on monitoring anything they desire or deem to be in 'the interests of the country' or the greater good. Most US employees surrender any rights to privacy when entering the workplace and, subsequently, utilising corporate assets or company property is subject to monitoring and audit (something that would not be tolerated in certain parts of Europe).

In some part of the United States, there are laws focusing on data protection: the State of California passed a law in 2003 (Data Breach Notification Law) that requires companies to notify consumers when personal information has been lost, stolen or compromised.

There are a number of other similar laws in other states that look to incorporate data protection and privacy; however, none of these are universal or adopted in majority fashion, leading to segregated and fractured data protection and privacy practices.

While no single framework exists to protect US citizens' privacy and personal information, a number of the acts and regulations that are focused on specific sectors or industries do look to incorporate such principles, albeit not their sole or primary focus.

These include (but are not limited to) the following.

Health Insurance Portability and Accountability Act (HIPAA) Privacy Rule

The HIPAA Privacy Rule is the first comprehensive Federal protection for the privacy of personal health information. The HIPAA Privacy Rule was enacted and endorsed by the US Congress in 1996, and is also known as the Standard for Privacy of Individually Identifiable Health Information. HIPAA provided the first nationally recognisable regulations for the use and/or disclosure of an individual's health information.

The HIPAA Privacy Rule defines how entities are permitted to process, use, or store personally identifiable health information or the PHI (Personal Health Information).

Note that HIPAA is only relevant for health-related information.

PHI is classified as any information which contains (or lists) information linked specifically to an individual, including health status, medical conditions, ailments, disabilities, provision of health care or payment for health care.

Entities required to adhere with HIPAA Privacy Rule are referred to as 'covered entities', and include the likes of health care clearinghouses, health insurers, medical service providers and organisations providing health care plans for employees.

The HIPAA Privacy Rule focuses on providing the following:

- giving patients control over the use of their health information;
- providing clearly stated rules for the use and/or disclosure of health records by relevant entities;
- establishing nationally applicable standards that healthcare providers are required to adhere to and comply with;
- limiting the use of PHI, and minimising opportunities of inappropriate disclosure;
- investigating compliance-related issues and ensuring violations are met with civil, or criminal penalties for violations.

Under HIPPA, a covered entity may disclose PHI to facilitate treatment, payment or health care operations, or if the covered entity has obtained specific authorisation from the individual themselves. When information is disclosed by the covered entity, best effort is required to only make available or disclose the minimum amount of information to fulfil its specified purpose.

As of 23 September 2009, all covered entities are required to notify patients of any security breaches involving their medical information. The Breach Notification Requirements are only concerned with the unauthorised acquisition, access, use or disclosure of unsecured PHI (an example of this would be a lost or stolen unencrypted laptop containing PHI).

United States Patriot Act

The US Patriot Act (342 pages, 15 statutes) was passed into law by Congress on 26 October 2001 following the terrorist attacks of 11 September 2001 (an extremely quick turnaround for such a substantial Act). The Patriot Act gives federal officials greater authority and ability to track, intercept and analyse communications for law enforcement and intelligence uses.

Aside from the national security focus, the Patriot Act also provides the Secretary of the Treasury with additional powers to address and combat corruption involving money laundering and related activities.

The Patriot Act looks to protect the United States borders from terrorists and those who target national security with the view of causing harm to US citizens. It created new crimes, new penalties and new procedural efficiencies for use against domestic and international terrorists (again all done in a space of under two months).

While many critics and privacy professionals state the Patriot Act goes too far in exposing sensitive and personal information that may not be relevant, others, such as the Department of Justice, hold reservations that the Act does not go far enough in assisting them to adequately protect the well-being and security of the United States and its people.

The following points in the Patriot Act are most relevant in terms of data privacy and Cloud Computing (other elements, such as money laundering, are not discussed, in order to maintain the focus of this publication).

Criminal investigations: tracking and gathering communications

The Federal Communications Privacy Law (separate from the Patriot Act; included for completeness) was developed to outline the measures and mechanisms for protecting the confidentiality of private telephone, face-to-face and technology communications. However, it does enable relevant authorities to identify and intercept 'criminal communications' for security purposes.

The privacy law gives authorities a specifically defined scope for electronic surveillance, and states that these are to be used as a last resort in serious criminal cases (many industry professionals question whether this is the case). This includes, but is not limited to:

- permitting trap and trace for electronic communications (most notably e-mails);
- authorising nationwide execution of court orders for pen registers (a device that captures dialling, routing, addressing or signalling information), trap and trace devices, and access to stored e-mail or communication records;
- treat stored voice-mail like stored e-mail (rather than like telephone conversations, whether live or not);
- permit authorities to intercept communications to and from a trespasser within a computer system (with the permission of the system's owner, i.e. telecom provider or similar);

- add terrorist and computer-related crimes to predicate offense list;
- promote co-operation and communication between various law enforcement and foreign intelligence investigators;
- establish a claim against the United States for certain communications privacy violations by government personnel and employees

Foreign intelligence investigations

The Patriot Act has also reduced some of the restrictions (previously many) on foreign intelligence gathering within the United States, thus affording the US intelligence and related law enforcement agencies access to vast amounts of information discovered, recorded and logged during criminal and other subsequent investigations.

While the following may not be immediately apparent due to the unknown levels of official/unofficial Cloud usage amongst foreign agencies, diplomats and personnel (whether organisational or personal Cloud usage), it incorporates the following:

- permits 'roving' surveillance;
- allows application for a Foreign Intelligence Surveillance Act (FISA) surveillance or search order, when gathering foreign intelligence is a significant reason for the application;
- authorises pen register and trap-and-trace device orders for e-mail, as well as telephone conversations;
- sanctions court-ordered access to any tangible item, rather than only business records held;

- expands the prohibition against FISA orders based solely on a US citizen's exercise of their First Amendment rights.

At the time of printing, The Patriot Act has caused some privacy concerns in the European Union, discouraging a move to the Cloud.

Who is subject to the Patriot Act?

All US citizens, personnel residing within the US and US-based or US-owned organisations are subject to the Patriot Act. This means they are allowed to be monitored and tracked by the FBI and CIA should they be suspected or be thought to pose a threat to the United States and its borders.

But that's not it! This might come as a shock to some, but any European (or other non-US) or owned data that is stored, processed or handled by a US-owned subsidiary or corporation is subject to the Patriot Act. Any US-owned organisation that touches data on your behalf will make you subject to the Patriot Act. To put it in context, Microsoft, Google, Amazon and all the other large Cloud providers are US-owned organisations, and by using these organisations (any use), you are subject to the Patriot Act unless otherwise specifically stated.

There are some Cloud providers that are specifically designing Clouds and measures to address these concerns from European and other international locations.

With no changes to the Patriot Act currently proposed (the Act was due to expire in 2005 and was extended, with Barack Obama subsequently extending it once more on 26 May 2011), it seems as if the Patriot Act is here to stay for some time, and for any organisations looking to understand which regulations they may be subjected to, the Patriot Act is most definitely an important consideration.

APEC Privacy Framework

In addition to the much publicised and hotly debated EU vs. US data protection/privacy laws and practices, we have the Asia Pacific Economic Cooperation (APEC) Privacy Framework. The APEC Privacy Framework aims to promote a 'flexible approach' to information privacy protection across the 21 APEC member economies – of which the USA is one.

The key 'spirit' of the Framework is to avoid the creation and introduction of unnecessary or hindering barriers to information flows.

While APEC member countries are predominantly focused on the partnership for trade and economic reasons, the Framework looks to enable the communication of information between these nations for these reasons. The following nations are all part of the APEC member programme: Australia, Brunei, Canada, Chile, China, Hong Kong (not a country, part of China), Indonesia, Japan, South Korea, Malaysia, Mexico, New Zealand, Papua New Guinea, Peru, Philippines, Russia, Singapore, Taiwan, Thailand, United States of America and Vietnam.

While the APEC Framework was created to provide clear guidance and direction on privacy issues to organisations within APEC economies, it does so by highlighting what are termed 'reasonable expectations' for privacy.

The APEC Framework outlines nine key principles including:

- *Preventing harm* This principle looks to prevent the misuse of personal information to individuals.

- *Notice* This principle looks to ensure that data collection principles are clear and transparent as to what data is being collected and for what purpose it is used. Notice also requires individuals to be notified of any disclosures to other personnel or organisations (i.e. data transfers or sharing with a third party or separate entity).

- *Collection limitations* This principle outlines requirements for information collection to be done by lawful and fair means (i.e. whenever possible, providing notice of the collection and obtaining consent from the individual).

- *Uses of personal information* Personal information collected should be only used to satisfy the purpose for which it was originally collected or other compatible purposes. This is subject to change if the following requirements are satisfied:
  - obtaining consent from the individual whose personal information is collected;
  - when it is necessary to provide a product or service specifically product requested by the individual; or
  - by the authority of law and other legal instruments, proclamations and pronouncements of legal effect.

- *Choice* Where possible, individuals should be provided with clear and easily understandable choices in relation to the collection, use and disclosure of their personal information.

- *Integrity of personal information* Personal information should be accurate, concise and up to date to for the purposes of use.

- *Security safeguards* Appropriate security safeguards or measures should be utilised to protect information against risks, such as loss or unauthorised access, destruction, use, modification or disclosure among others.

  Levels of security should be proportional to the likelihood (what are the chances of the risk being exploited or realised?) and severity (how could this impact on the individual / organisation?) including the sensitivity of the information (health records / financial information / other).

  Best practice would dictate this should be subject to periodic reviews to keep in line with any changes.

- *Access and correction* This principle stipulates specific conditions of access and correction of information by the individual. It includes obtaining a copy of the information requested, and having the information rectified, completed, amended or deleted (where relevant).

- *Accountability* This principle ensures the information controller should be accountable for complying with the afore mentioned Principles from the collection of information through to the end of its life cycle.

International privacy at a glance (USA/EU/APEC)

Is it really the Europeans leading the USA and APEC in terms of privacy? For many privacy and data protection purists, this is the belief. While many professionals and businesses are quick to defend and utilise European privacy as a 'streamlined or uniform approach', it is worth noting that a single 'European Privacy Law' does not exist, and the

EU Privacy Directive is merely a list of principles that European nations should abide by.

Ultimately, the European Privacy Directive acts predominantly as a guideline or standard for European nations to follow, but not necessarily an 'all encompassing' rule or set of requirements. Add the complication that each of these nations has its own national laws with local agencies interpreting and enforcing those laws.

Currently, there are major variations from country to country, depending on their culture, legacies and history with transparency and privacy.

Depending on who you speak to, some are in favour of the approach taken by US multinational entities, others in favour of UK-based firms, and others preferring the German organisations' approach.

Privacy is ultimately a human right in some jurisdictions, with it being considered a privilege in others.

Privacy and data protection are just some of the regulations and frameworks that make up a plethora of compliance and regulatory headaches for those looking to make the move to Cloud Computing, and with no current solution in sight.

Guidelines for success

No silver bullet currently exists to simplify and deal with the challenges faced by those organisations looking to adopt and utilise Cloud Computing effectively, In line with relevant laws, regulations and requirements, the following points should be reviewed and explored as a starting point wherever possible:

- Consider the possible implications for processing/exporting of data to certain geographic locations or territories.
- Take all reasonable and appropriate steps to ensure that trans-border flows of personal data (including transit through other countries) are uninterrupted and secure.
- Where possible, restrict flow of data between countries and locations that contradict or violate domestic data protection/privacy regulations in your own location.

  There are a number of locations in which no legislation or requirements exist for the protection of personal data/information.

- Beware and understand any government or international relations becoming strained. There is significant risk storing, transmitting or processing data in a location or jurisdiction that is currently experiencing tension, strained relations or military action with your government or nation.
- Avoid complications and creation of a mesh of various restrictions, policies, practices and frameworks, which become an inhibitor for the organisation itself. Be conscious, realistic and pragmatic in your approach to develop a fit-for-purpose workaround or solution to support the overall business objectives.

In summary

This chapter was a high-level overview to illustrate some of the many challenges organisations will face relating to privacy and data protection from an international perspective. There are a number of substantial publications specialising in far more detail in the various areas and elements discussed in this chapter.

If you are unsure of the effect these elements relating to international Cloud Computing may have for your organisation, we would advise and encourage further research and engagement with suitably qualified and experienced professionals specialising in these areas to assist.

Additional resources

European Data Protection Directive

ec.europa.eu/justice/policies/privacy/index_en.htm

www.dataprotection.ie/

www.ico.gov.uk

United States Patriot Act

www.justice.gov/archive/ll/highlights.htm

epic.org/privacy/terrorism/hr3162.html

HIPAA

www.hhs.gov/ocr/privacy/

APEC Privacy Framework

apec.org/About-Us/About-APEC/Fact-Sheets/APEC-Privacy-Framework.aspx

CHAPTER 11: EVALUATING COMPLIANCE IN THE CLOUD

Compliance overview

Compliance from a definitions perspective would be defined as 'conforming to a rule, such as a specification, policy, standard or law' – these are typically external to the organisation.

In many real-world situations and environments, the above definition is often expanded, and tends to include additional operational risks and additional regulations, thereby extending the notion 'compliance' to other operational risk assessments and other frameworks or internal processes.

Compliance can be across any number of business units, functions or departments with a varying degree of requirements, measurement or frequency for assessment and adherence.

Regulations have grown in breadth due to fraud and abuse over the past 10 to 12 years, leading to a need for businesses to ensure a certain level of compliance in order to operate in the global markets. Many of these are highly intricate standards and frameworks that are combined and weighted with other overlapping or supplementary regulations and guidance frameworks.

The following are an example of some regulatory requirements:

- Sarbanes-Oxley Act (SOX)
- FISMA
- Gramm-Leach-Bliley Act (GLBA)

- COBIT
- C-Sox (Canada)
- Payment Card Industry Data Security Standard (PCI DSS)
- Health Information Portability & Accountability Act (HIPAA)
- various NIST Requirements
- ISO27001/27002
- ISO9001
- EU Data Protection Directive
- US Patriot Act
- ISAE 3402 (Formerly SAS 70)
- service level agreements.

In today's highly regulated business world, there is simply no place for businesses to hide regarding their compliance obligations, especially those requirements that have been around for some time. This could include the measurement, communication and reporting of compliance to a number of different bodies or entities where relevant.

Depending on the relevant industries and locations that an organisation operates within will dictate which regulatory requirements are applicable.

For example, a financial services organisation may have any number of frameworks, standards or regulations to adhere to, while a utilities or educational institute may have a completely different list of requirements to fulfil. The same might be relevant for an e-commerce trader accepting online payments in Bermuda, or a medium-sized electrical supplies manufacturer trading in Boston – no two organisations are the same and, as such, need to be aware of all regulatory requirements.

Both Cloud providers and Cloud customers will have to fully understand regulatory requirements prior to the migration to Cloud, as this may be a significant factor in relevant contracts or SLAs.

If recent developments are anything to go by, we may well see specific Cloud deployments tailored to address regulatory requirements (such as PCI DSS), which may provide peace of mind to customers who face these challenges. However, as with all outsourcing or third-party agreements, you cannot outsource your compliance obligations! You remain responsible regardless, and this should never be seen as an easy solution or quick fix.

Need for compliance functions

Compliance has historically been a closely aligned function with the legal team, and will continue to operate in this fashion for the foreseeable future.

While no generic compliance programme or standard compliance framework exists, the role of compliance within an organisation is never to be underestimated.

The following are some of the typical activities performed by a compliance function for an organisation:

- developing and administering policies and procedures to comply with legal and regulatory requirements;
- developing and administering training programmes for employees and contractors covering regulatory requirements;
- assisting employees ongoing legal and regulatory requirements;

- monitoring of systems for adherence and breach of organisational policies;
- assisting (and possibly leading) any investigations and breaches of legal and regulatory requirements;
- reporting and engaging with executives on the compliance posture of the organisation;
- liaising with regulators in relation to regulatory matters.

Compliance may also be responsible for the co-ordination of activities related to the collection of evidence and other materials required in the event of an investigation.

Compliance vs. internal audit

What is the difference? Surely they are both focused on ensuring policies, procedures, standards and regulations are adhered to?

Not necessarily so. Typically internal audit is a risk control function that is responsible for testing internal control systems, reporting and recommending improvements related to these. While there are a number of elements that overlap with compliance, internal audit typically conducts an audit (usually a sample of controls), where the ongoing monitoring and follow-up actions are performed by compliance on a regular or ongoing basis.

Value of compliance done correctly

Compliance, like most other business functions, is not immune from tight funding, budget cuts, competition for organisational resources and reallocation of staff. Even in today's highly regulated industries, compliance is also facing battles to obtain sufficient, or additional, budgets to illustrate adherence to relevant requirements. They are forced to review, revise and streamline the way in which they operate.

Illustrating and reporting value for money, or return on investment, is always a challenging and sometimes fruitless task. So how can compliance executives state their case to get attention during the corporate budgeting process?

Change brings about opportunities!

Since 2009, I have seen many organisations and departments look at the way their units have functioned proactively for the first time in many years.

Having looked at operations and structures from an objective viewpoint (with slight pressure to do so!), many companies have introduced efficiencies and innovative ideas to assist with reduced budgets and funding.

Never more so than now – opportunities to utilise innovative, cutting-edge and developing technologies, such as Cloud Computing, are becoming more readily available on a daily basis. What exactly is meant by this?

Cloud Computing presents possible opportunities once thought of unimaginable to improve assurance, transparency, reporting and accountability through consolidated, centralised and operated platforms.

Included in this are some of the measures being made available by Cloud providers that would simply not have been affordable or practical prior to the Cloud Computing era.

The opportunity also exists for entities to negotiate additional measures and capabilities as part of the contracts and relevant SLAs.

Cloud first – compliance second?

While most organisations (including Cloud providers) are adapting to the changes introduced by Cloud Computing, it is certainly a case of Cloud first, everything else second (for the time being at least!). Cloud is still immature by most business standards, and is still developing and adapting at a rapid rate (public, private, hybrid and community Clouds are all changing).

Until such time as service offerings, Cloud providers and other factors become more constant and settled, it is not likely that compliance will be driving development of Cloud service offerings.

Worth noting and a key consideration is that most regulatory and international compliance frameworks are still coming to terms with the intricacies and challenges that Cloud Computing introduces. These include international data flows, data ownership, monitoring, logging and reporting among many others.

How these are going to be addressed from a regulatory perspective remains to be seen, but ignorance of unknowns will not suffice.

What changes for compliance functions?

As with traditional or in-house computing structures, organisations will be required to display compliance or alignment with frameworks. In order for this to be completed, the following questions should be answered as a minimum:

- What are the regulatory challenges or shortfalls for using a specified Cloud service or Cloud provider?

- How will cross-border data flows be controlled, if at all (*see Chapter 10*)?
- Are there clear lines of separation and responsibility outlining requirements for the Cloud service provider and customer?
- Are there any additional providers that you may not be aware off (third-party providers may outsource aspects or elements to other organisations)?
- What capabilities or facilities exist for the Cloud provider to prove compliance, including reporting, evidence and adherence to best practice?
- What mechanisms are in place to support transparency between Cloud provider and customer (scheduled reporting, unscheduled reporting, proactive communication of changes, etc.)?

By understanding the above, these should act as the starting point for revising current compliance practices prior to a possible move to Cloud Computing.

Who is responsible for what?

Traditionally, compliance functions or departments would work with various departments and where relevant third-party providers to co-ordinate and facilitate regulatory requirements for the overall business. Whether these skills were readily available internally, or contracted from an external body, organisations typically had the luxury of obtaining relevant information from within their current premises or various geographic locations.

How much has changed? Is this still possible? It's the company's information – surely compliance reporting should be a given? Perhaps – but time to delve a little deeper!

Compliance strategy and framework

With potential moves to new locations and boundaries (if any such exist in the Cloud!), the requirement exists to fully understand and review the alignment and structure of existing compliance, risk and governance functions within the organisation.

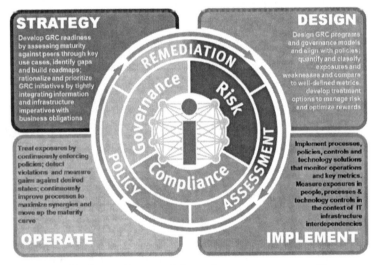

Figure 13: Compliance, risk and governance readiness

While many would have seen the evolution of Cloud Computing over recent times, few have proactively incorporated Cloud Computing into their compliance strategy frameworks. It may well be a fruitful exercise to review the compliance (and other strategy documents) to ascertain how Cloud Computing has incorporated (if at all) the organisation's two to five year plan. If your company's compliance strategy has not taken into account Cloud Computing, now may be the time to take a step back and revise accordingly.

The domino effect

What are the interdependencies between compliance and other functions – does each action have a reaction, possibly impacting on others? Why does this impact on all governance, risk and compliance functions?

As necessary as each component is as a stand-alone function, the dependency and reliance on the other functions as business enablers or requirements is stark and never to be underestimated. These functions, like security, are only as good as the information they receive and, as such, can easily impact on each other.

Lack of co-ordination, co-operation and communication can result in significant (in some cases severe) actions being experienced.

Governance

Governance typically focuses on the alignment of internal requirements, such as corporate policies, business objectives and strategy.

Like so many other factors of Cloud Computing, governance can be one of the most crucial components or aspects to ensuring a successful Cloud programme! Without proactive, efficient and measurable governance across all areas of business, it is not possible to fully understand and interpret challenges, issues or results effectively.

Lack of governance almost always leads to lack of funding, and a lacklustre compliance or security programme!

Governance becomes a culture within an organisation, and without this culture being managed and operated effectively can have a detrimental effect on other areas or aspects of the business.

The importance and reliance on governance is never to be underestimated and for that reason, it has a full chapter dedicated to it (*see Chapter 3*), where a number of possible frameworks, methodologies and options are discussed in detail.

If you happened to skip over *Chapter 3*, it is well worth seeing which aspects of governance you might look to incorporate into your Cloud Computing programme or strategy.

Regulatory challenges

While regulations may dictate the manner in which business operations are conducted, they form an integral part of daily, weekly and monthly requirements. With no let-up in the number of regulations, laws and directives that organisations are required to adhere to, this area will only increase over the coming years.

In some jurisdictions and industries, the cost of maintaining compliance with regulations, such as Sarbanes-Oxley, PCI DSS and others, can be from thousands to millions of dollars. Failing to adhere or maintaining compliance with such regulations can have a detrimental effect on the company's reputation, share price, stock values and other qualitative elements.

Even with numerous cyber attacks, data breaches, insider threats and other high-profile incidents, many sizable organisations have illustrated that while they may have been compliant, this does not necessarily mean secure! All the regulations and frameworks in the world cannot ensure complete security or an all-encompassing system.

Threats will continue to evolve and morph at a rapid rate, and while the intentions of regulatory requirements are not to deal with every possible threat, they look to apply a standardised approach to elements, which may cause considerable cost, harm or inconvenience to those affected.

Cost of compliance (or non-compliance!)

While the cost of compliance may often be the subject of much debate from boardrooms to compliance teams, the cost of compliance is often significantly lower than the cost of non-compliance. Depending on the size, nature and complexity of business operations, compliance can be as high as 1% of total earnings – no small sum of money!

So which is it – how much will it cost to be compliant, and how much could non-compliance cost? Is it as simple as a cost-benefit analysis?

In a recent study of 46 multinational organisations conducted by TripWire Inc. and the Ponemon Institute, it found that for multinational organisations who do not comply with relevant legislations and regulations, the cost of non-compliance is 2.65 times the cost of compliance. Simply put, most organisations will end up paying just under three times the amount in follow-up actions, penalties and other associated costs than if compliance measures had been implemented initially.

Additionally, organisations that are non-compliant will typically experience a higher number of incidents, more disruptions to business operations and greater costs in dealing with those incidents (the domino effect).

Cloud Computing standards and compliance

While a number of Cloud Computing security standards are currently being drafted, proposed and developed, there remains somewhat limited guidance or frameworks for Cloud providers and customers alike to obtain assurance as to levels of security, governance, risk and compliance. At present there is currently no de facto or clear leader for organisations to adopt to satisfy external requirements or the ongoing bombardment of surveys, questionnaires or audits from prospective customers.

While it may take some time before de facto Cloud standards are used universally, the following ISO and ITU-T (formerly CCITT) standards are slowly gaining momentum and being adopted by Cloud Computing providers and customers alike.

These standards continue to attract attention for their ability to measure and assess adherence and compliance for services and Cloud environments:

- ISO/IEC 27017 – Cloud Computing Security and Privacy Management System-Security Controls
- ISO/IEC 27036-x – Information security standard for supplier relationship related to Cloud supply chain
- ITU-T X.ccsec – Security guidelines for Cloud Computing in telecommunications

- ITU-T X.srfcts – Security requirements and best-practice framework for Cloud Computing telecommunication service environments
- ITU-T X.sfcse – Security functional requirements for Software-as-a-Service application environments.

While the above-mentioned standards are currently somewhat immature in their footprint and international recognition, the adoption of ISO27001 (Information Security Management System) continues to increase.

Service providers are continually being asked to illustrate their security posture to current and prospective clients regarding information security, compliance and network management. For the foreseeable future, it is likely that ISO27001 will continue to be adopted by large-scale providers as a popular (and relatively cost-effective) way of displaying independent verification and adherence to best practice.

Recent trends and surveys

A number of recent studies, conducted in Europe and the United States, have stated that security, privacy and compliance concerns are the number one barrier for adoption of Cloud Computing.

In a recent study from Deloitte and CIOnet in Europe, it was revealed that those who had decided not to adopt Cloud Computing had the following concerns:

- 20% of respondents cited insufficient data security and risk availability;
- 17% of respondents cited legal or compliance issues;

- 14% of respondents cited risk of losing governance or control.

In a similar survey conducted on over one thousand US-based professionals by the Ponemon Institute (sponsored by Vormetric Inc.), the following results were published:

- 56% of IT practitioners said that security concerns will *not* keep their organisations from adopting Cloud services;
- 52% of compliance executives felt their organisations had sufficient policies and procedures to enable safe and secure use of Cloud ;
- 21% of compliance officers said they were responsible for defining security requirements in the Cloud;
- 31% of respondents said their major Cloud providers used encryption to protect data from insider threats.

Results from these surveys seem to indicate that while security and compliance tend to attract universal concerns from organisations and professionals alike, the rate of Cloud Computing adoption continues to increase significantly.

Recent discussions among certain sectors of the Cloud Computing community seem to indicate that specific Cloud deployments may soon be tailored to address aspects such as the US Patriot Act, the EU Privacy Directive, PCI DSS and others, by ensuring the infrastructures, platforms and software offerings take into account requirements from certain regulations and legislations, and streamline the process for their customers.

Soon it may well be possible to obtain IaaS (and other offerings) that are focused on aiding or fulfilling PCI DSS requirements from a technical perspective.

Segregation of duties

While much of the focus of compliance relies heavily on documentation, reporting, metrics, measurement and ongoing monitoring, a key compliance and security component that could be overlooked by many organisations moving to Cloud-based services or environments is that of 'segregation of duties' (SOD – also referred to as 'separation of duties').

SOD divides or segregates the responsibility of a critical task that could have significant impact on operations among different people and introduces a second step to check or approve against fraud or error.

Many regulatory and internal audit functions in enterprises worldwide have specific and very necessary requirements for the use of SOD.

Best practice, coupled with requirements from regulations and legislation, such as Sarbanes-Oxley and PCI DSS, tend to focus heavily on SOD as a key component or aspect in daily business activities to reduce risks and threats to key business activities and systems.

SOD in Cloud environments

Traditional designs and architectures vary from organisation to organisation. When moving or utilising Cloud environments, these new environments should take into account SOD, and the manner in which these will be incorporated, designed, reviewed and exercised prior to a full move to Cloud environments.

Depending on the Cloud service selected or environment utilised will determine the impact or requirement to revise controls accordingly. Whether it is a private Cloud or a public Cloud, SOD will most likely be used in some form.

Private Cloud uses could include appropriate change controls and change management to sensitive data. Others might be data access, identity and access management, as well as other financial transactions or payments.

Public Cloud uses could include IT security-related activities, such as policy, logging, monitoring, alert changes and others (who, what, where etc.).

Other changes involving SOD may include IT operations activities, encryption mechanisms and associated key changes, financial transactions exceeding a certain amount, along with other interdepartmental actions.

The above represent a small number of examples, which may be applicable to your organisation. As with all changes, sufficient time and resources should be assigned to allow the process or procedure to be implemented, operated, matured and improved.

Where to start?

Over the past 12 months, significant contributions have been made by many industry professionals to assist those in the Cloud Computing decision-making process.

The following documents and materials should provide valuable reading for those currently venturing down the decision-making path:

Cloud Security Alliance

The Cloud Security Alliance (CSA) is a not-for-profit organisation with a mission to promote the use of best practices for providing security assurance within Cloud Computing, and to provide education on the uses of Cloud Computing to help secure all other forms of computing. The CSA is led by a broad coalition of industry practitioners, corporations, associations and other key stakeholders.

Relevant guidance materials include:

- Security Guidance for Critical Areas of Focus in Cloud Computing v.3.0
- Cloud Controls Matrix v.1.2
- various white papers and research articles.

https://cloudsecurityalliance.org/

ENISA

The European Network and Information Security Agency (ENISA) is the European Union's response to cybersecurity issues affecting the EU. As such, it is the pacesetter for information security in Europe and a centre of expertise. Their objective is to make ENISA's website the European hub for exchange of information, best practices and knowledge in the field of information security.

Relevant guidance materials include:

- Cloud Computing Risk Assessment
- Cloud Computing Information Assurance Framework.

www.enisa.europa.eu/

NIST

National Institute of Standards and Technology was founded in 1901. NIST is a non-regulatory federal agency within the US Department of Commerce. NIST's mission is to promote US innovation and industrial competitiveness by advancing measurement science, standards and technology in ways that enhance economic security and improve quality of life.

Relevant guidance materials include:

- NIST Special Publication 500-293, US Government Cloud Computing Technology Roadmap, Release 1.0 (Draft), Volume I High-Priority Requirements to Further USG Agency Cloud Computing Adoption
- NIST Special Publication 500-293, US Government Cloud Computing Technology Roadmap, Release 1.0 (Draft), Volume II Useful Information for Cloud Adopters.

www.nist.gov/itl/cloud/

ISACA

ISACA acts as an independent, non-profit, global association. It engages in the development, adoption and use of globally accepted, industry-leading knowledge and practices for information systems.

Relevant guidance materials include:

- IT Control Objectives for Cloud Computing: Controls and Assurance in the Cloud
- Cloud Computing: Business Benefits With Security, Governance and Assurance Perspectives.

https://www.isaca.org

References

- 'The True Cost of Compliance', Ponemon Institute (January 2011).
- 'Cloud Adoption Study', Deloitte & CIOnet (May 2011).
- 'Data Security in the Cloud: Survey of US IT Operations, IT Security and Compliance Practitioners', Ponemon Institute.
- Security Guidance for Critical Areas of Focus in Cloud Computing v.3.0.

Definitions and references from:

https://www.isaca.org

www.nist.gov/itl/Cloud /

https://cloudsecurityalliance.org/

www.enisa.europa.eu/

CHAPTER 12: WHERE CLOUD COMPUTING IS HEADING

The industry enthusiasm for Cloud Computing indicates that it addresses elements of IT that suffer from fundamental dissatisfaction.

IT is commonly regarded as unresponsive, slow-moving, expensive and difficult to work with.

Cloud Computing, with its rapid provisioning, pay-as-you-go pricing and user self-service, addresses these pain points.

Any time a new solution neatly addresses the shortcomings of a given situation, it seems obvious that it will be embraced immediately.

The overwhelming enthusiasm directed toward Cloud Computing suffers from only one reservation: security. Many IT professionals react to the promise of Cloud Computing with a 'yes, but' attitude. 'Yes, Cloud Computing sounds great, but what about knowing if my company's data is safe from access by provider personnel?'

This book has been devoted to addressing the numerous concerns people have about Cloud Computing that commonly are labelled as 'security', but often fall into other areas like governance and compliance. We have taken a comprehensive approach and addressed all of the topics that people lump under the topic of 'Cloud security'. We hope our analysis has, if not solved the issues under these topics, at least provided mechanisms, so that they may be approached and mitigated sufficiently, such that IT organisations can move forward with their Cloud Computing initiatives.

This poses a question: what will Cloud Computing look like when the issue of security is no longer considered a reason to delay moving forward?

Here are a few predictions.

Much greater growth in Cloud Computing adoption than anyone predicts One of the paradoxes of life is that, as something gets less expensive, one uses more of it. So much so that, despite the reduced cost, overall spend grows due to increased consumption volumes. This will certainly pose a challenge to IT organisations and their parent companies. Assumptions about the appropriate IT budget ('Our industry spends 3% of revenues on IT') will be rethought as less-expensive computing fosters vastly increased use. Staffing levels in IT organisations are likely to grow as business units seek to fund new initiatives because of the convenience and cost-effectiveness of Cloud Computing.

Scale challenges infrastructure The boom in computing described above will be accompanied by an enormous growth in scale. More network traffic, more computing and especially more storage will cause many companies to outgrow their data centres. Look to Cloud providers to continue to build gigantic data centres to support customers who have burst beyond the walls of their internal computing environments.

Increased focus on IT costs Earlier, we noted that most IT organisations are unable to evaluate their true cost of providing service due to the fact that budgets are commonly distributed among different organisations: facilities, IT, finance, even HR. The difficulty of bringing the total costs into a single comprehensive budget means it is extremely difficult for IT to create an accurate picture of the cost of providing a fine-grained service, like the monthly cost of a single gigabyte of storage. Cloud providers, on the other hand, have built their businesses on fine-grained services and transparent pricing. Business consumers of IT services are likely to compare the two providers and insist that IT offer the same type and transparency of pricing. This will cause IT to perform a complete rethink of budgeting, pricing and offerings. A side effect of this business-unit pressure is that IT will move to standardised offerings delivered through automation. Business users seeking customised solutions will find steep premiums tacked on to their bill to support personalised service.

IT becomes the business The reduced cost and associated growth of IT will extend into solutions aimed at mobile devices and new types of business offerings. IT will move from a role of automating internal business processes to implementing new business initiatives. IT will finally get its wish of a seat at the table; in fact, IT may be at the head of the table.

Mixed environments call for comprehensive security solutions Privacy requirements, enormous growth and cost pressure will all force IT to move to a new perspective on computing environments. Internal and external environments will be considered equal, with the decision of where to deploy an application driven by an assessment of security needs, easy scalability requirements and TCO. IT organisations will seek security solutions that can comfortably span both internal and external environments and provide a comprehensive solution.

12: Where Cloud Computing is Heading

The history of IT has been remarkable. Ever cheaper, always being delivered in smaller form factors, being applied to new problems and forever confounding practitioner assumptions and projections. Cloud Computing is squarely within this tradition and represents the latest platform revolution. No one can know with certainty what will become of Cloud Computing, but it seems safe to say that it will be just as unpredictable as its computing forbears. Thomas Watson, Jr., CEO of IBM, once famously predicted that the total global market for computers would be five. Five!

From our perspective, it seems likely that all of the predictions about Cloud Computing are likely to fall just as short as Watson's prediction in terms of accuracy – and just as revolutionary as what really transpired in the computing industry.

Thank you!

ITG RESOURCES

IT Governance Ltd. sources, creates and delivers products and services to meet the real-world, evolving IT governance needs of today's organisations, directors, managers and practitioners.

The ITG website (*www.itgovernance.co.uk*) is the international one-stop-shop for corporate and IT governance information, advice, guidance, books, tools, training and consultancy.

www.itgovernance.co.uk/Cloud-computing.aspx is the information page on our website for Cloud Computing resources.

Other websites

Books and tools published by IT Governance Publishing (ITGP) are available from all business booksellers and are also immediately available from the following websites:

www.itgovernance.co.uk/catalog/355 provides information and online purchasing facilities for every currently available book published by ITGP.

www.itgovernance.eu is our euro-denominated website which ships from Benelux and has a growing range of books in European languages other than English.

www.itgovernanceusa.com is a US$-based website that delivers the full range of IT Governance products to North America, and ships from within the continental US.

www.itgovernanceasia.com provides a selected range of ITGP products specifically for customers in South Asia.

www.27001.com is the IT Governance Ltd. website that deals specifically with information security management, and ships from within the continental US.

Pocket guides

For full details of the entire range of pocket guides, simply follow the links at *www.itgovernance.co.uk/publishing.aspx*.

Toolkits

ITG's unique range of toolkits includes the IT Governance Framework Toolkit, which contains all the tools and guidance that you will need in order to develop and implement an appropriate IT governance framework for your organisation. Full details can be found at *www.itgovernance.co.uk/products/519*.

For a free paper on how to use the proprietary Calder-Moir IT Governance Framework, and for a free trial version of the toolkit, see *www.itgovernance.co.uk/calder_moir.aspx*.

There is also a wide range of toolkits to simplify implementation of management systems, such as an ISO/IEC 27001 ISMS or a BS25999 BCMS, and these can all be viewed and purchased online at *http://www.itgovernance.co.uk/catalog/1*.

Best Practice Reports

ITG's range of Best Practice Reports is now at *www.itgovernance.co.uk/best-practice-reports.aspx*. These offer you essential, pertinent, expertly researched information on a number of key issues including Web 2.0 and Green IT.

Training and consultancy

IT Governance also offers training and consultancy services across the entire spectrum of disciplines in the information governance arena. Details of training courses can be accessed at *www.itgovernance.co.uk/training.aspx* and descriptions of our consultancy services can be found at *http://www.itgovernance.co.uk/consulting.aspx*. Why not contact us to see how we could help you and your organisation?

Newsletter

The governance of IT is one of the hottest topics in business today, not least because it is also the fastest moving, so what better way to keep up than by subscribing to ITG's free monthly newsletter *Sentinel*? It provides monthly updates and resources across the whole spectrum of IT governance subject matter, including risk management, information security, ITIL and IT service management, project governance, compliance and so much more. Subscribe for your free copy at: *www.itgovernance.co.uk/newsletter.aspx*.

CPSIA information can be obtained at www.ICGtesting.com
Printed in the USA
BVOW081311091212

307689BV00007B/142/P